THE POETRY MAKERS

BOOK 4

The six full-page pictures on pages 36, 68, 100, 154, 196 and 216 of this book are reproductions (much reduced) of etchings by Anthony Currell from 'Wales', a series of twelve prints on the theme of the Welsh miner. The prints are published by Editions Alecto Ltd, 27 Kelso Place, London, W.8, and the reproductions in this book appear by kind permission of Editions Alecto and of the artist.

The Poetry Makers

a graded anthology of poetry
for Secondary schools
chosen by

JAMES McGRATH M.A.

Deputy Headmaster
St Pius' Secondary School
Glasgow

BOOK 4

HEINEMANN EDUCATIONAL BOOKS
LONDON

Heinemann Educational Books Ltd
22 Bedford Square, London WC1B 3HH

LONDON EDINBURGH MELBOURNE AUCKLAND TORONTO
HONG KONG SINGAPORE KUALA LUMPUR NEW DELHI
IBADAN NAIROBI JOHANNESBURG KINGSTON
EXETER (NH) PORT OF SPAIN

ISBN 0 435 14573 8

First published by The Bodley Head 1968
First published by Heinemann Educational Books Ltd
in association with The Bodley Head 1969
Reprinted 1972, 1974, 1978, 1984

Printed and bound in Great Britain by
Spottiswoode Ballantyne Ltd, Colchester and London

ACKNOWLEDGMENTS

We would like to thank the following for permission to reprint copyright material:

Faber & Faber Ltd. for 'James Honeyman' by W. H. Auden from *Another Time*; the author for 'The Black Ape' by Leo Aylen; John Murray Ltd. for 'Seaside Golf' and 'A Subaltern's Love Song' by John Betjeman from *Collected Poems*; A. D. Peters & Co. Ltd. for 'Incident in Hyde Park, 1803' by Edmund Blunden; the author for 'The Life Style' by Edwin Brock; The Hogarth Press Ltd. for 'Culloden: The Last Battle' by George Mackay Brown from *The Year of the Whale*; 'Mia Carlotta' by T. A. Daly from *Selected Poems of T. A. Daly*. Copyright 1936 by Harcourt, Brace & World, Inc., renewed © 1964 by Thomas A. Daly Jr. and reprinted by permission of the publishers; The Hutchinson Publishing Group for 'The Stay-at-Home' by Marjorie Driscoll; the author for 'Landscape as Werewolf' by William Dunlop; Faber & Faber Ltd. for 'Journey of the Magi' by T. S. Eliot from *Collected Poems 1909–1962*; the author for 'Night of the Scorpion' by Nissim Ezekiel from *The Exact Name* published in 1966 by the Writers' Workshop, Calcutta; William Heinemann Ltd. for 'Secret Police' by G. Rostrevor Hamilton from *Collected Poems*; the Trustees of the Estate of Thomas Hardy, Macmillan & Co. Ltd. and the Macmillan Company of Canada Ltd. for 'The Rash Bride', 'One Who Married Above Him' and 'The Sacrilege' by Thomas Hardy from *The Collected Poems of Thomas Hardy*; Gerald Duckworth & Co. Ltd. for 'A Newcomer' by Graham Hough from *Legends and Pastorals*; Faber & Faber Ltd for 'View of a Pig', 'Pike' and 'Esther's Tomcat' by Ted Hughes from *Lupercal*; the author for 'The Gunboat' by Robert Gittings; Mr Robert Graves for ' "The General Elliott" ' by Robert Graves from *Collected Poems 1959* (Cassell); The Hutchinson Publishing Group and P.E.N. International for 'Julia Smeaton' by Ada Jackson from *New Poems* (1957); Curtis Brown Ltd. for 'Earthquake' by James Kirkup from *The Prodigal Son* (O.U.P.); Laurence Pollinger Ltd. and the Estate of the late Mrs Frieda Lawrence for 'Snake' by D. H. Lawrence from *The Collected Poems of D. H. Lawrence* (Heinemann); André Deutsch Ltd. for 'The fox-coloured pheasant enjoyed his peace' by Peter Levi; the executors of the late F. L. Lucas for 'Spain 1809' by F. L. Lucas; the author for 'Wild Sports of the West' by John Montague first published in *The Listener* and subsequently in *Poisoned Lands* (MacGibbon & Kee); Faber & Faber Ltd. for 'The Cleggan Disaster' by Richard Murphy from *Sailing to an Island*; Mr Milton Waldman, literary executor of the late Robert Nichols, for 'Battery Moving up to a New Position from Rest Camp: Dawn' by Robert Nichols from *Poems* (Chatto & Windus); Chatto & Windus Ltd. and Mr Harold Owen for

'Dulce et Decorum Est' by Wilfred Owen from *Poems* and 'Anthem for Doomed Youth' by Wilfred Owen from *The Collected Poems of Wilfred Owen*, edited by C. Day Lewis; the author for 'The Dorking Thigh' by William Plomer from *Collected Poems by William Plomer* (Cape); Scorpion Press for 'Your Attention Please' by Peter Porter from *Once Bitten, Twice Bitten*; David Higham Associates Ltd. for 'For Johnny' from *Collected Poems* (Putnam); the author for 'A Mountain Stream' by Peter Russell; the author for 'The Young Labourers' by Arthur Wolseley Russell; the author for 'The New Admission' by Olive M. Salter (this poem first appeared in *Nine* no. 7 Summer 1950, edited by Peter Russell); David Higham Associates Ltd. for 'The Phoenician Woman' by Clive Sansom from *The Witnesses and Other Poems* (Methuen); the author for 'The Rear-guard' by the late Siegfried Sassoon; the author for 'Autobiographical Note', 'Gunpowder Plot', 'Romantic Suicide' and 'Incendiary' by Vernon Scannell; Oxford University Press for 'The Trap' by Jon Stallworthy from *Out of Bounds;* the author fro 'Neighbour' and 'Hillside Burial' by Storey from *The Listener* and *The Review of English Literature* respectively; Rupert Hart-Davis Ltd. for 'Cynddylan on a Tractor' by R. S. Thomas from *Song at the Year's Turning*; the author for 'African Beggar' by Raymond Tong; Faber & Faber Ltd. for 'Ballad' by Henry Treece from *The Black Seasons*; Angus & Robertson Ltd. for 'The Fishers' by Brian Vrepont; Macmillan and Co. Ltd. and The Macmillan Company of Canada Ltd. for 'Au Jardin des Plantes' by John Wain from *Weep Before God*; the author for 'Anecdote' by C. Henry Warren from *The Listener*; Faber & Faber Ltd. for 'The Collier' by Vernon Watkins from *Ballad of the Marie Lwyd*; Centaur Press Ltd. for the extract from 'A Tale for the Fall of the Year' by Margaret Stanley-Wrench as it appeared in *Prose and Verse Readings—Summer Term 1962* (B.B.C.); Angus & Robertson Ltd. for 'The Killer' by Judith Wright; Mrs W. B. Yeats and Macmillan & Co. Ltd. for 'Down by the Salley Gardens', 'For Anne Gregory', 'The Host of the Air' and 'To an Isle in the Water' by W. B. Yeats from *Collected Poems of W. B. Yeats*.

We have been unable to trace the copyright holders of the following poems and would be grateful for any information which would enable us to do so: 'Light' by F. W. Bourdillon; 'The Thing' by Theodore Roethke.

FOREWORD

A new series of poetry anthologies for secondary schools must, in an increasingly crowded field, have something particular to say for itself. THE POETRY MAKERS is the fruit of some fifteen years' experience in the teaching of poetry to boys and girls of secondary school age, and is designed as staple fare for these pupils.

The series is graded—a delicate matter, and one on which no two lovers of poetry can ever quite agree. But, again in the light of experience, I believe that users of this series will find that there is to be found in each book an overall appropriateness for the age group on which they can rely, and to which their students will respond. I have rejected arrangement by themes, a system which prejudices the student's reponse to the poem itself, and one which has been recently much overdone. Instead. I have juxtaposed the poems—by length, by subject matter, and by tone of voice—in the belief that such an arrangement stimulates awareness, and fosters discrimination. The order of poems within each book again reflects an idea of grading, and if the user does want poems arranged by themes he will find ample material for the class to group poems in this way *for themselves*. It will also be found that each of the first three books is in a real sense a preparation for the next. Events, moods and images which are treated at one level in, say, Book 1, will be found to recur at a new level of maturity in Book 2. The same will be found with the poets themselves, who are asked to say new things at new levels of sophistication as the series progresses.

A final word about my ultimate canon of selection: when faced with the choice, I have always preferred the concrete image to the abstract, the eventful to the static. These are books to be enjoyed, and a powerful factor to this end is that in every poem something of interest takes place.

Brief notes will be found at the end of certain poems. These are either glosses on archaisms, diction and dialect, or explanations of the poem's setting in time and place, or of its basis in history and legend.   J. McG.

CONTENTS

Where no author is given the poem is anonymous

9

† *indicates an extract, or that the text has been cut*

▶ A Newcomer

I saw her on the pavement's edge,
Not timid, half-smiling at the crowd
That tumbled round; she did not budge;
Only her eyes moved.

A dusky little muzzle like some pretty
Small animal crept from a sun-spotted
Thicket by mistake to this grey city.

African maybe, or West Indian.
Just stumbled out of childhood, staring
Into a blank unknown,
And quite unfearing.

I never thought before
So quicksilver a wisp could stay so still
So separate, until
What I wished not to see I saw—
Her small black-kitten life was maimed and hobbled;
She leant on crutches; the girl was crippled.

Three times a loser, then.
Her childhood lost, and nothing else begun;
Lost too the Caribbean sun;
And half her strength and proper lightness gone.

Yet in her face among that grey-faced crowd
The three lost suns still glowed.

GRAHAM HOUGH

▶ James Honeyman

JAMES HONEYMAN was a silent child
He didn't laugh or cry;
He looked at his mother
With curiosity.

Mother came up to the nursery,
Peeped through the open door,
Saw him striking matches
Sitting on the nursery floor.

He went to the children's party,
The buns were full of cream;
Sat dissolving sugar
In his tea-cup in a dream.

On his eighth birthday
Didn't care that the day was wet
For by his bedside
Lay a ten-shilling chemistry set.

Teacher said: 'James Honeyman's
The cleverest boy we've had,
But he doesn't play with the others
And that, I think, is sad.'

While the other boys played football
He worked in the laboratory
Got a scholarship to college,
And a first-class degree.

Kept awake with black coffee,
Took to wearing glasses,
Writing a thesis
On the toxic gases.

Went out into the country,
Went by Green Line bus,
Walked on the Chilterns,
Thought about Phosphorus.

Said: 'Lewisite in its day
Was pretty decent stuff,
But under modern conditions
It's not nearly strong enough.'

His Tutor sipped his port,
Said: 'I think it's clear
That young James Honeyman's
The most brilliant man of his year.'

He got a job in research
With Imperial Alkali
Said to himself while shaving:
'I'll be famous before I die.'

His landlady said: 'Mr Honeyman,
You've only got one life,
You ought to have some fun, Sir.
You ought to find a wife.'

At Imperial Alkali
There was a girl called Doreen,
One day she cut her finger,
Asked him for iodine.

'I'm feeling faint,' she said.
He led her to a chair,
Fetched her a glass of water,
Wanted to stroke her hair.

They took a villa on the Great West Road,
Painted green and white;
On their left a United Dairy,
A cinema on their right.

At the bottom of his garden
He built a little shed.
'He's going to blow us up,'
All the neighbours said.

Doreen called down at midnight
'Jim dear, it's time for bed.'
'I'll finish my experiment
And then I'll come,' he said.

Caught influenza at Christmas,
The Doctor said: 'Go to bed.'
'I'll finish my experiment
And then I'll go.' he said.

Walked out on Sundays,
Helped to push the pram,
Said: 'I'm looking for a gas, dear;
A whiff will kill a man.

I'm going to find it,
That's what I'm going to do.'
Doreen squeezed his hand and said:
'Jim, I believe in you.'

In the hot nights of summer
When the roses were all red
James Honeyman was working
In his little garden shed.

Came upstairs at midnight,
Kissed his sleeping son,
Held up a sealed glass test-tube,
Said: 'Look, Doreen, I've won!'

They stood together by the window,
The moon was bright and clear.
He said: 'At last I've done something
That's worthy of you, dear.'

Took a train next morning,
Went up to Whitehall
With the phial in his pocket
To show it to them all.

Sent in his card,
The officials only swore:
'Tell him we're very busy
And show him the door.'

Doreen said to the neighbours:
'Isn't it a shame?
My husband's so clever
And they didn't know his name.'

One neighbour was sympathetic,
Her name was Mrs Flower.
She was the agent
Of a foreign power.

One evening they sat at supper,
There came a gentle knock:
'A gentleman to see Mr Honeyman.'
He stayed till eleven o'clock.

They walked down the garden together,
Down to the little shed:
'We'll see you, then, in Paris.
Good night,' the gentleman said.

The boat was nearing Dover,
He looked back at Calais:
Said: 'Honeyman's N.P.C.
Will be heard of, some day.'

He was sitting in the garden
Writing notes on a pad,
Their little son was playing
Round his mother and dad.

Suddenly from the east
Some aeroplanes appeared,
Somebody screamed: 'They're bombers!
War must have been declared!'

The first bomb hit the Dairy,
The second the cinema,
The third fell in the garden
Just like a falling star.

'Oh kiss me, Mother, kiss me,
And tuck me up in bed
For Daddy's invention
Is going to choke me dead!'

'Where are you, James, where are you?
Oh put your arms around me,
For my lungs are full
Of Honeyman's N.P.C.!'

'I wish I were a salmon
Swimming in the sea,
I wish I were the dove
That coos upon the tree.'

'Oh you are not a salmon,
Oh you are not a dove;
But you invented the vapour
That is killing those you love.'

'Oh hide me in the mountains,
Oh drown me in the sea.
Lock me in the dungeon
And throw away the key.'

'Oh you can't hide in the mountains,
Oh you can't drown in the sea,
But you must die, and you know why,
By Honeyman's N.P.C.'

W. H. AUDEN

▶ Seaside Golf

How straight it flew, how long it flew,
   It clear'd the rutty track
And soaring, disappeared from view
   Beyond the bunker's back—
A glorious, sailing, bounding drive
That made me glad I was alive.

And down the fairway, far along
   It glowed a lonely white;
I played an iron sure and strong
   And clipp'd it out of sight,
And spite of grassy banks between
I knew I'd find it on the green.

And so I did. It lay content
   Two paces from the pin;
A steady putt and then it went
   Oh, most securely in.
The very turf rejoiced to see
That quite unprecedented three.

Ah! seaweed smells from sandy caves
   And thyme and mist in whiffs,
In-coming tide, Atlantic waves
   Slapping the sunny cliffs,
Lark song and sea sounds in the air
And splendour, splendour everywhere.

JOHN BETJEMAN

▶ A Tale for the Fall of the Year

Twenty years ago, when you could have held our village
In your hand, and seen the squat, white clapboard houses
Like a crowd in corduroy smocks, ridged roof and shingle
Pulled tight down over their eaves, you'd have judged it
     right
As a small, sly place; the windows, with blinds or shutters
Drawn, seemed to make the village stare down its nose,
And the crooked shacks were nudging neighbours tattling,
Seeing the seams of your stockings, the track you was takin'
And the course of your life wasn't straight. Oh, we was
     censorious,
Virtuous, and better than we ought to be!
All but Amos. Ah! but then he was an idiot.
He used to make baskets for a living. Queer, those hands of
     his,
Brown and big as his head, nipped in and out
Of the wicker like two weasels; the finger nails
Were smooth as new-shelled nuts. Sometimes he'd mend
Chairs with dried rushes, dry and bitter rushes
Whispering of treachery, emptiness and man's ending,
Down there by the river. Makes me shudder thinking of it,
Moving snake-like through the slime. Yet Amos paddled
Barefoot in the ice-blue water many a morning,
And laughed as if the grip of it round his ankles
Had been the light touch of a boy's cold hand.
Where did he live? Look, that's his shack yonder,
Mostly broken up now, smothered by the morning glories'
Pouting cotton-white trumpets, and the cockscomb crimson
Of the palm-wide creeper leaves. Someone's old barn.
He lived there with bats, the shoals of mice, and birds.
Never lonely—his candle guttered from a beam.
He slept on corn shucks, huddled in sacks and blankets,
And cobwebs clung to his hair, powdering it mildly

With a faint mildewed greyness, as if he mouldered there.
I can remember the broad blur of his face.
Loose swinging arms that moved as if they was separate
Beasts on a leash, not limbs linked to a man.
But his eyes, ah, they were beautiful and frightening,
Wide, but like holes in him, nothing at the end of their
    blueness.
Not even a beast's eyes are bottomless, like his were.
No, he wasn't dangerous, a simple creature, the children
Loved him; his bigness acted like as if it fenced them
From danger, and yet, though he was man-size, never
Did he hold them back, or give reasons, or read a lesson,
But walked side by side with them, fitting his clumsy feet
Into the small prints they made . . .
                    They'd talk a little louder.
'Come on, Amos, come *on*, we're goin' to the mountains'—
Their voices tugged at him; into the storm-blue distance
They'd go, yet no-one noticed. Amos was becoming
Part of the landscape, like a gopher or the stippled feather
Of an owl, bark-brown in the branches. Not even the gossips
Cocked an eye at his step or pulled aside the curtains.
It was as if we breathed him, sensed him, forgot him.
He didn't count. And no-one minded the children
Making him the hub of their games, no more than if
They'd played round the stub of a tree or an old stone.
I remember one time I saw them, in the fall sunlight
Playing around his shack. They'd picked the seed pods
Of honesty or moonwort, round, parchment-coloured
Pods as big as dollars, and in between
The papery husks is a slip of moon-white silk.
The children use it as money. I'd hear them shouting
'I've a dollar twenty, how much have you got, Amos?'
And he'd be sitting, counting, grinning as a dog does,
As if basking in firelight. Sometimes he'd go
To the stores, for flour or molasses, and pass those silver
Seeds in place of cents. But no one bothered.

How could you make him understand? And which
Rang truest, white nickels, or the shimmering coins of
    moonwort?
The storekeepers smiled, touched their heads, and nodded,
Then swept up the worthless pods; the wind snatched them
Away to the darkness as a starved dog trails its bone,
And Amos, walking home on the stilts of his own shadow
Was happy as only a man without thought can be.

Yes, I can still see him, far off, way back in the past
Like a clear drawing, in bright and rain-fresh colours,
With the children around him, the grass, sharp autumn
    green,
The mushroom white of the honesty seeds, an innocent
Hoard piled up, over them the clear hard blue
Of the sky, as wide and empty as the eyes of the idiot,
And across the hut, with the wet red of blood,
The trailing vine leaves glistening in the sun.
Is he still here? What, Amos? Sometimes I think
I see him, his homespun worn thin, and bleached as grey
As the skeleton leaves when winter frosts have frayed them.
Sometimes I think I hear his shuffling feet,
But it's only a leaf, or a dog scuffling in the thickets,
And his stubble hair turns to tufts of thistledown blowing—
That was the way he went, as if he melted
Like a beast into the landscape. No one knew
When they first missed him. It was winter, children all
    penned
In separate houses, most folk indoors. We guessed
Amos had stocked up with flour and corn and molasses,
And was sealed up snug as a dormouse in his shack.
No, we never worried, not until the deep snows
Came, and then we turned anxious. Didn't seem natural
That drifts should lie up so high against the shack,
Not thawed by a chimney, and not the chink of a window
To break the idiot whiteness, only the hairsbreadth

Fragile sputtering footprints of birds across it,
And the clubbed, clove-dark spoor of a marten or wild cat
    trekking
Up the roof as if it was a hill. We started digging
Faster, faster, as if frightened now, as if wanting
To let in air and light to what we'd find.
And gradually the cold, and more than the cold sunk
    inwards
And pinched us and numbed us, till we was all ache and a
    hankering
Emptiness of spirit. Oh, yes, we found him,
In the pitiless brightness of snowlight probing through the
    window,
Sprawled like an old heap of mangels. Dead, yes, dead.
Someone had beaten out life like dust out-a mats
With a great cudgel, and over everything
The stupid white moons of the honesty seeds was scattered
As if someone had gone rantin' mad. Tramps, we reckoned,
Then all of us saw, sudden and sharp, the way
You do sometimes, a picture of tragedy
Before it happens, the characters set out
Just so it would work out that way. Against the cedar-wood
Glow of the inn, the lamplight warm, the mugs
Of ale brown as huckleberries or the knuckles holdin' 'em
And Amos, his broad face bursting open with its seed-
White smile, boasting of the bags of dollars in his cabin.
We knew, we nodded, the silver was the seeds of moonwort.
We smiled at his simplicity, our grins
A noose of friendship linking us into the circled
Lamplight, and the warmth of knowing, and the safety of
    wholeness.
Amos was the outsider who made us kindred,
Who gave our unsteady steps a moment's firmness,
Who shut out the greater dark for an instant. Pity
For him, in his innocence, and his lopped being
Turned us into gods in the oil light of a bar parlour.

But there, in the shadow, two tramps, their faces scooped
    hollow
By a rage of greed, gaped and watched, and their eyes
Burned red like those of starved dogs slavering at food.
We were too complacent, too loud in our own laughter,
And too satisfied to see the three outsiders,
Amos, in his lonely, clouded dark, and the tramps
Like men ringed round by fire, their backs to flame,
And no way out, no let up, no escape.

Yes, I reckoned that's how it happened. No, we never caught
    'em.
Amos was buried in the churchyard. Someone keeps
His stone clean white as the moonwort. Sometimes children
Lay a bunch of wilting daisies there. We cut
The grass. What else can we do? He lies there easy.

MARGARET STANLEY-WRENCH

▶ Married to a Soldier

The pride of all the village,
The fairest to be seen,
The pride of all the village
That might have been a queen,
Has bid good-bye to neighbours
And left the dance and play
And married to a soldier
And wandered far away.

Her cottage is neglected,
Her garden gathers green,
The summer comes unnoticed
Her flowers are never seen;
There's none to tie a blossom up
Or clean a weed away;
She's married to a soldier
And wandered far away.

The neighbours wonder at her
And surely well they may,
To think one so could flatter
Her heart to go away.
But the cocked hat and feather
Appeared so very gay,
She bundled clothes together
And married far away.

JOHN CLARE

▶ Julia Smeaton

I was a parson's daughter and
The house where I was bred
Stood hard against the church, so that
We neighboured with the dead.

I married with a parson and
For forty years and three
We moved from dreary vicarage
To draughtier rectory.

Thro' pinchfist griping parishes
To livings fat with dues;
My house for ever set by tombs
And grave-mould on my shoes.

Old gravestones marked my garden's end;
Times in the sleepless dawn
It seemed the mounds were waves that must
Engulf my little lawn.

The moon would make the crosses dance
And fissures open wide,
While dead folk beat upon our doors
And begged to come inside.

Year by long year I prayed escape,
Full forty years and more;
But life brought none, and death hath laid
Us closelier than before.

Now cold I dwell among the cold,
My gravestone, small and white,
The first to catch the parson's eye,
The last he sees at night;

The nearest to the wicket gate,
Hard by the rectory,
Where many a parson's wife shall think
She shuts the latch on me,

But wake, as I woke, in the grey,
To blench and snatch her breath,
As will I nill I in my turn
I stare her to her death.

ADA JACKSON

▶ Ye Flowery Banks
o' Bonnie Doon

Ye flowery banks o' bonnie Doon,
　　How can ye bloom sae fair!
How can ye chant, ye little birds,
　　And I sae fu' o' care!

Thou'll break my heart, thou bonnie bird
　　That sings upon the bough;
Thou minds me o' the happy days
　　When my fause Luve was true.

Thou'lt break my heart, thou bonnie bird
　　That sings beside thy mate;
For sae I sat, and sae I sang,
　　And wist na o' my fate.

Aft hae I roved by bonnie Doon
　　To see the woodbine twine;
And ilka bird sang o' its love,
　　And sae did I o' mine.

Wi' lightsome heart I pu'd a rose,
　　Frae aff its thorny tree;
And my fause luver staw the rose,
　　But left the thorn wi' me.

ROBERT BURNS

ilka: every
staw: stole

▶ Esther's Tomcat

Daylong this tomcat lies stretched flat
As an old rough mat, no mouth and no eyes.
Continual wars and wives are what
Have tattered his ears and battered his head.

Like a bundle of old rope and iron
Sleeps till blue dusk. Then reappear
His eyes, green as ringstones: he yawns wide red,
Fangs fine as a lady's needle and bright.

A tomcat sprang at a mounted knight,
Locked round his neck like a trap of hooks
While the knight rode fighting its clawing and bite.
After hundreds of years the stain's there

On the stone where he fell, dead of the tom:
That was at Barnborough. The tomcat still
Grallochs odd dogs on the quiet,
Will take the head clean off your simple pullet,

Is unkillable. From the dog's fury,
From gunshot fired point-blank he brings
His skin whole, and whole
From owlish moons of bekittenings

Among ashcans. He leaps and lightly
Walks upon sleep, his mind on the moon.
Nightly over the round world of men,
Over the roofs go his eyes and outcry.

TED HUGHES

Grallochs: disembowels

▶ The Cleggan Disaster

from *Sailing to an Island.*

Five boats were shooting their nets in the bay
After dark. It was cold and late October.
The hulls hissed and rolled on the sea's black hearth
In the shadow of stacks close to the island.
Rain drenched the rowers, with no drying wind.
From the strokes of the oars a green fire flaked
And briskly quenched. The shore-lights were markers
Easterly shining across the Blind Sound.

Five pieces of drift-net with a mesh of diamonds
Were paid from each stern. The webbed curtains hung
Straight from the cork-lines, and warps were hitched
To the strong stems, and the pine oars boarded.
The men in the boats drew their pipes and rested.

The tide fell slack, all the breakers were still.
Not a flicker of a fish, only the slow fall
Of the ocean there drawing out the last drops of sleep.
Soon they could feel the effort of the ebb
Yearning at the yarn, twitching their mooring-stones
Stealthily seawards. Two boats began to haul.

From the bows of a boat in the centre of the bay
Concannon watched and waited. On each far wing
He heard them hauling. He held in his hand
The strong hemp rope which stretched from the cork-line
So that his fingers could feel the cord throb
If the shoal struck the nets. But so far, nothing.

Why had those others hauled? They were old
And experienced boatsmen. One man on the quay

warps: tow ropes   *stems:* bows

At Bofin warned him, 'Sharpen your knife,
Be ready for trouble, cut away your nets.
Your crew is too young.' Were they going home?
Would the night not remain calm enough to fill
The barrels in their barns with food for the winter?

He was sure of his boat, though small, well built.
Her ribs and her keel were adzed out of oak,
Her thole-pins were cut out of green holly,
And the grapnel was forged by the Cleggan smith.
Since the day she was launched, she had been lucky.

He was doubtful of his crew: three men and a boy
Who needed the money. Their land was poor,
But they had no heart for this work on water . . .

As luck began to load the farthest nets,
And the green mackerel river raced through the water,
Crossed over the gunwales, and jetted fire
In the black braziers of the rolling bilges.

He thought, as the lucky stream continued to flow,
'There are three more pieces of net to be hauled.
If we're too greedy, we could sink the boat.
We have enough now to row home safely.
Cut them in time and return in the daylight.
Darker it's getting, with a north-west wind.' . . .

A storm began to march, the shrill wind piping
And thunder exploding, while the lightning flaked
In willow cascades, and the bayonets of hail
Flashed over craters and hillocks of water.
All the boats were trapped. None had reached the pier.
The target of the gale was the mainland rocks.

The men began to pray. The stack-funnelled hail
Crackled in volleys, with blasts on the bows
Where Concannon stood to fend with his body
The slash of seas. Then sickness surged,
And against their will they were griped with terror.

He told them to bail. When they lost the bailer
They bailed with their boots. Then they cast overboard
Their costly nets and a thousand mackerel.

She was drifting down the sound, her mooring-stone
    lifted
By the fingers of the tide plucking at the nets
Which he held with scorching hands. Over and over
He heard in his heart, 'Keep her stem to the storm,
And the nets will help her to ride the water;
Meet the force of the seas with her bows,
Each wave as it comes.' He'd use the knife later.

Down in the deep where the storm could not go
The ebb-tide, massive and slow, was drawing
Windwards the ninety-six fathom of nets
With hundreds of mackerel thickly meshed,
Safely tugging the boat off the mainland shore.
The moon couldn't shine, the clouds shut her out,
But she came unseen to sway on his side
All the waters gathered from the great spring tide . . .

The oarsmen were calling Concannon to let go,
Take it easy for a while. Let the boat drift
To the Cleggan shore, down wind, till they touch land.
Even there, if they died, it would be in a bay
Fringed with friends' houses, instead of in the open
Ocean, where the lost would never be found,
Where nothing is buried, no prayers are said.
Concannon silenced them, and stiffened his hold.

Twice the lightning blinked, then a crash of thunder.
Three cliffs of waves collapsed above them, seas
Crushed in his face, he fell down, and was dazed . . .

He knelt against the stem, his hands bleeding,
His eyes, scalded by the scurf of salt,
Straining to give shape to the shadows they saw
That looked like men in the milder water.
One of the crew said he heard his brother
Shouting for help, two oars away,
Yet when he hollered, there was no reply.
In a lightning flash, a white hand rose
And rested on the gunwale, then slowly sank.

Down the valleys of this lull, like a black cow
In search of her calf, an upturned hull
Wallowed towards them. Her stem had parted.
All hands must have been lost. She hoved to his side
And almost staved him. Were the men inside?
Those who had thrown him his ropes from the quay?
The one who had warned him about his crew?
No help for them now. With his foot on her planks
He fended her off. As she bore away,
Her keel like a scythe cut a clear white swath
Through the gale's acres. Then a great sea crossed.

On the far side, as he nipped among white horses
Bolting towards him, under the streamers of manes
And the quick hoof-lash, he still headed the storm:
The chargers' lances hurtled with little harm
Through the icy air, while their hooves plunged on.

Now, though sea-boils encrusted his eyes,
He saw the Lyon Light, in spurts when they rode
Upon grey shoulders, flicker from white to red.
Lumps of water licked across tidal shallows.

They cantered at walls, and then faced hills.
The horses stampeded, as lanes closed ahead
In a white chalk-cliff. Rolled under horses
With manes in their mouths, their bones smashed,
Their blood washed away . . . Yet the cliff was passing,
The water rose to the thwarts. They went on bailing.

What were those lights that seemed to blaze like red
Fires in the pits of waves, lifted and hurled
At the aching sockets of his eyes, coals that lit
And expired in the space of a swell's slow heave?
'Am I going blind? *Am I going blind*?' he thought.
'Look at that wave. How it sharpens into a rock.

WATCH THAT ROCK. GET READY TO JUMP. It's
    gone.
Now *there's* a light . . . count the seconds: a slow pulse.
I can see that light from my own back door,
Slyne Head, never so high, such piercing brightness.
Where has it gone? Spears in hundreds are hurtling
Against my head. Was it south of us it shone?' . . .

Lights flickered and vanished. Like a brown bear
Hugging a tree, he clung to the stem, his eyes closed.
The boy whispered. 'There's rocks to leeward.'
'What rocks do you think?' another asked.
'Dog Rock, I think, I fished here last summer.'
Concannon opened his knife: 'I'm cutting the nets.'
Piece by piece he slashed, but he had to tear
The clinging hanks with his finger bones, at last
He severed the rope, their guide on that dire sea-road,
And sank to his knees. The boatsmen rowed,
Backwards, falling away, her stem still to the storm,
With their eyes fixed on the faint lamps
That led across calm waters to Cleggan Quay.

It was three o'clock when she nudged the steps.
Safe on the stone bollards they fastened their ropes.
The full moon was whitening the ribs of hulks
In the worm-dark dock. The tide was flowing
As they trudged to the village. His crew helped him:
The sea had not claimed him, she had left him blind.

They met a crowd
      at the gates of the fish-store.
Bodies of fishermen
      lay on the floor on boxes.
There was blood on their faces.
      Three were dead.
Boats came ashore on shingle
      with all hands lost.
As the day dawned,
      gap after gap was filled . . .
The funeral boats brought over
      the bodies found,
But most were carried away
      on the great ebb-tide.
From the village of Rossadillisk
      they lost sixteen
And from the Bofin nine.
      One man above all was blind.

In a common grave
      that was dug in the sand-dunes
Close to high-water mark
      but leagues from low springs
They laid side by side
      the deal-board coffins
Lowering them on ropes,
      then shovelled the fine sand
Which whisperingly slid
      round their recent companions,

And sometimes the shovels met
        with a knelling clang
While in shifts they worked
        till the mound was raised.

After the prayers were said
        and the graveyard closed
Concannon was counting
        the fifty steps to his house,
Working out sounds,
        the sea-fall on the beach.
Would the islanders ever again
        dare to fish?
When he'd mastered this dark road,
        he himself would ask
To be oarsman in a boat,
        and mend the nets on land.
The croak of a herring-gull
        tolled across the sky.
An oyster-catcher squealed.
        Shoals broke on the bay.
The flood tide rose and covered
        the deserted strand . . .

RICHARD MURPHY

▶ Cynddylan on a Tractor

Ah, you should see Cynddylan on a tractor,
Gone the old look that yoked him to the soil;
He's a new man now, part of the machine,
His nerves of metal and his blood oil.
The clutch curses, but the gears obey
His least bidding, and lo, he's away
Out of the farmyard, scattering hens.
Riding to work now as a great man should,
He is the knight at arms breaking the fields'
Mirror of silence, emptying the wood
Of foxes and squirrels and bright jays.
The sun comes over the tall trees
Kindling all the hedges, but not for him
Who runs his engine on a different fuel.
And all the birds are singing, bills wide in vain,
As Cynddylan passes proudly up the lane.

R. S. THOMAS

▶ The Killer

The day was clear as fire,
the birds sang frail as glass,
when thirsty I came to the creek
and fell by its side in the grass.

My breast on the bright moss
and shower-embroidered weeds,
my lips to the live water,
I saw him turn in the reeds.

Black horror sprang from the dark
in a violent birth,
and through its cloth of grass
I felt the clutch of earth.

O beat him into the ground,
o strike him till he dies,
or else your life itself
drains through those colourless eyes.

I struck again and again;
slender in black and red
he lies, and his icy glance
turns outward, clear and dead.

But nimble my enemy
as water is, or wind;
he has slipped from his death aside
and vanished into my mind.

He has vanished whence he came,
my nimble enemy,
and the ants come out to the snake
and drink at his shallow eye.

JUDITH WRIGHT

▶ The Gunboat

This is a story of love and death, and a lake
So deep, the fishermen dropping their weighted lines
Never touch stone or rocky sand: for the earth
Breaks hollow there, some buried rift in the crust
Enough to cavern a monster or swallow a ship,
And this is the story.

                            A hundred years ago,
Italy, singing country of lemon and vine,
Stank like a dungeon. Uniforms strutted and clicked,
Foreigners gave the orders, prison or death,
Austrian voices, Austrian soldiers, Austria
Flying its clawing eagle flag in the blue
Darkened the sunlight. Only one half of the lake
Among the mountains still was free; there a man
Could steal a boat, and skilfully paddle, and land
Where a shaded light gave signal, so to escape
The tyrant bloodhounds leashed by the grim police
To the free side of the lake with peace and laughter,
Until the gunboat came.

                        That was a stroke
To startle and crush. 'We'll show these lying Italians.'
So the Austrian engineers, sweating and blond,
Dragged the bright sections by mule-back over the mount-
    ains,
Fitting the parts like a jigsaw, and there it lay,
Squat scorpion, grey paint sizzling in the heat,
Bristling with shells and ugly turrets, a warship
Steaming its menacing plume on the peaceful lake.
That was an end of resistance: few tried it. The boat
Slipping across in the darkness, pretending to fish,
Seeking a friendly lantern, was suddenly framed
In the white shock of a searchlight: all at once spoke

The guns in an orange bellow. Some broken planks
And a fisherman's bonnet, pitiable disguise,
Were all that traced the spot, as the swordfish monster
Circled once, then steamed away, satisfied.

Now in Verona, Austrian-held, the Count,
Young, handsome, the secret hope of many in Italy,
Took a bride, she too Italian, and known
Like him to hate the tyrants. Then, what horror
To loyal friends and Italians, the Count announces
His honeymoon plans, to charter the Austrian gunboat
And cruise on the lake, to use their murder-ship
As a pleasure steamer. Austrian permission
Was easily granted for this, a fine demonstration
Better even than guns, to show the Italians
Their noble leader forgot all plot of revolt
In love, for love would tread the enemies' deck
And fly the flag of his love at their conquering masthead.
But the Italians—what fury and scorn when they saw
Not only the Count and his bride aboard, but found
Themselves the guests, feast under awnings, the guns
Pushed back, festooned with pennants and flowers, the ship
Blazing with lights beneath a velvet sky,
And the Austrian crew, drinking the wedding toast,
While the Count and his bride, like a slender lily, stood there
Receiving and bowing among this foreign court
Of men who had sent Italian blood to death.

And yet this was not the worst. For every nightfall
The gunboat anchored abreast a different town
On the rocky shore of the lake. The Count's invitation
Summoned aboard all families; loathing, they came
To another feast, each longer than the first
More lavish with wine and healths to the happy couple,
Drunk deep by guffawing Austrian sailors, drunk
Sour between gritted teeth by the bitter Italians,

41

Who stayed no more than for sober politeness, then left
Muttering as their servants rowed them ashore.
Still smiling, the two young lovers stood at the rail
Waving good-bye, blind, infatuate, while
The drunken Austrians finished the food and the wine.
So the wedding cruise went on, one week, two,
Three, till the angry guests at each fresh night
Murmured openly now that the young Count's fortune
Would soon be spent, and many wished him that evil,
Till the garlanded gunboat came to the deepest part
Of all the long lake. Here hundreds of guests were bidden
From miles around. The invitations were pressing.
The guns on the boat, though shrouded, still were guns.
No one dared to refuse. But rage in their hearts
Grew high at the gross, most huge of festivities;
When early the foreign crew were drunk, insulting,
Staggering, and the Count, like a courteous host,
Took the chief Austrians below, put them to bed
With lengthy care, returned to the upper deck
With bland apologies, while the Italians glared
At him and his bride, and barely pressed the glasses
To moisten their lips.

                       And so it was that soon
Only Italians were left on the deck. And these,
The last of their vile invaders now drunk below,
Needed no cause to stay: nor did the Count
Nor the bride detain such a scowling company,
Feeling contempt in each brief touch of handshake,
Seeing the flash in the eye, as more than one guest
Spat as he swung down the gunboat side, and dropped
Into the boats that swiftly rowed them ashore.
And all, looking back with curses, saw, as always,
The Count and the young slim girl, his arm round her waist,
Standing there at the stern-rail, silent, motionless,
Alone now.

Grumbling, the guests moved, up mountain paths
And dark herb-scented walks, each one toward home,
Leaving the black lake. Then, with a blinding flash
Never yet known on that water, the lake lit up,
And a bellowing roar like a beast in agony, hit
And hammered the cliff with echoes. Everyone turned
To the ship—the ship! There, over the deepest grave
Of the whole deep lake, in a burial sheet of flame
Tilted the ship on its death-dive, the flower-fed guns
Exploding in horrible heat, destroying itself
With its own infernal engines. For the Count, who took
Such time below with the drunk incapable crew,
Had stoked red-hot the boilers, let out the water,
And primed the ship to a pulse of death. And still
Ringed with that terrible flame, the two at the rail
Stood clasped, the Count and his bride. They had done,
     from the first,
What they meant to do. They had put the devilish boat
In the deepest hole of the lake. They had done it alone,
Without help of friends, without love of friends, alone
With only their love to join them. And, joined in love,
The watchers upon the hillside saw how that honeymoon
Ended: the small groups everywhere fell to their knees
In congregation beneath the church of the stars:
'Gesu, Maria, what kind of a love was here!'

That was a story of love and death and a lake:
Of a lake so deep, and a love so deep, the mind
Cannot imagine, nor any eye trace its depth,
So deep it lies beyond dredging: not even a nail
From a rusty boat nor a ring from a wedding finger.

ROBERT GITTINGS

▶ Counsel to Girls

Gather ye rosebuds while ye may,
   Old Time is still a-flying:
And this same flower that smiles to-day
   To-morrow will be dying.

The glorious lamp of heaven, the sun,
   The higher he's a-getting,
The sooner will his race be run,
   And nearer he's to setting.

That age is best which is the first,
   When youth and blood are warmer;
But being spent, the worse, and worst
   Times still succeed the former.

Then be not coy, but use your time,
   And while ye may, go marry:
For having lost but once your prime,
   You may for ever tarry.

ROBERT HERRICK

▶ Your Attention Please

Your Attention Please—
The Polar DEW has just warned that
A nuclear rocket strike of
At least one thousand megatons
Has been launched by the enemy
Directly at our major cities.
This announcement will take
Two and a quarter minutes to make,
You therefore have a further
Eight and a quarter minutes
To comply with the shelter
Requirements published in the Civil
Defence Code—section Atomic Attack.
A specially shortened Mass
Will be broadcast at the end
Of this announcement—
Protestant and Jewish services
Will begin simultaneously—
Select your wavelength immediately
According to instructions
In the Defence Code. Do not
Take well-loved pets (including birds)
Into your shelter—they will consume
Fresh air. Leave the old and bed-
Ridden, you can do nothing for them.
Remember to press the sealing
Switch when everyone is in
The shelter. Set the radiation
Aerial, turn on the geiger barometer.
Turn off your Television now.
Turn off your radio immediately
The services end. At the same time
Secure explosion plugs in the ears
Of each member of your family. Take

Down your plasma flasks. Give your children
The pills marked one and two
In the C.D. green container, then put
Them to bed. Do not break
The inside airlock seals until
The radiation All Clear shows
(Watch for the cuckoo in your
Perspex panel), or your District
Touring Doctor rings your bell.
If before this your air becomes
Exhausted or if any of your family
Is critically injured, administer
The capsules marked 'Valley Forge'
(Red pocket in No. 1 Survival Kit)
For painless death. (Catholics
Will have been instructed by their priests
What to do in this eventuality.)
This announcement is ending. Our President
Has already given the orders for
Massive retaliation—it will be
Decisive. Some of us may die.
Remember, statistically
It is not likely to be you.
All flags are flying fully dressed
On Government buildings—the sun is shining.
Death is the least we have to fear.
We are all in the hands of God,
Whatever happens happens by His will.
Now go quickly to your shelters.

PETER PORTER

▶ For Johnny

Do not despair
For Johnny-head-in-air;
He sleeps as sound
As Johnny underground.

Fetch out no shroud
For Johnny-in-the-cloud;
And keep your tears
For him in after years.

Better by far
For Johnny-the-bright-star,
To keep your head,
And see his children fed.

JOHN PUDNEY

▶ The Dorking Thigh

About to marry and invest
Their lives in safety and routine,
Stanley and June required a nest
And came down on the 4.15.

The agent drove them to the Posh Estate
And showed them several habitations.
None did. The afternoon got late
With questions, doubts, and explanations.

Then the day grew dim and Stan fatigued
And disappointment raised its head,
But June declared herself intrigued
To know where that last turning led.

It led to a Tudor snuggery styled
YE KUMFI NOOKLET on the gate.
'A gem of a home,' the salesman smiled,
'My pet place on the whole estate;

It's not quite finished, but you'll see
Good taste itself.' They went inside.
'This little place is built to be
A husband's joy, a housewife's pride.'

They saw the white convenient sink,
The modernistic chimney piece.
June gasped for joy, Stan gave a wink
To say, 'Well, here our quest can cease.'

The salesman purred (he'd managed well)
And June undid a cupboard door.
'For linen,' she beamed. And out there fell
A nameless Something on the floor.

48

'Something the workmen left, I expect.'
The agent said, as it fell at his feet,
Nor knew that his chance of a sale was wrecked.
'Good heavens, it must be a joint of meat!'

Ah yes, it was meat, it was meat all right,
A joint those three will never forget—
For they stood alone in the Surrey night
With the severed thigh of a plump brunette . . .

Early and late, early and late,
Traffic was jammed round the Posh Estate,
And the papers were full of the Dorking Thigh
And who, and when, and where, and why.

A trouser button was found in the mud.
(Who made it? Who wore it? Who lost it? Who knows?)
But no one found a trace of blood
Or her body or face, or the spoiler of those.

He's acting a play in the common air
On which no curtain can ever come down.
Though YE KUMFI NOOKLET was shifted elsewhere
June made Stan take a flat in town.

WILLIAM PLOMER

▶ The Stay-at-Home

The village knew her as a faithful wife,
Low-voiced and patient with her husband's ways,
Busy through all the uneventful days
With small home duties that made up her life.

She'd married young; a quiet, sober man,
Not one to talk much; satisfied to sit
And smoke his pipe of evenings; drowse a bit,
His slow thoughts on the little store he ran.

The times were hard the year they married, so
They took no wedding-trip, but waited, till
The years had somehow drifted by, and still
It never seemed to be the time to go.

So they lived together he and she,
The children grew up, married, went away.
Things went along from quiet day to day—
Then she died suddenly.

And when they came to tidy up, they found
Down, in the bottom of her box of scraps
A child's geography with coloured maps,
A shell that made a curious murmuring sound,

A steamship guide with pictures crude and blurred
Of white ships sailing by a palm-green shore—
Java, Sumatra, Bangkok, Singapore—
A strange, bright feather from some foreign bird;

A bit of paper daubed with gilt and red
That once had wrapped a pound of Chinese tea;
A yellow clipping: 'How to Dress at Sea.'—
'What queer trash some folks keep around!' they said.

MARJORIE CHARLES DRISCOLL

▶ Battery Moving up to a New Position from Rest Camp: Dawn

NOT a sign of life we rouse
In any square close-shuttered house
That flanks the road we amble down
Toward far trenches through the town.

The dark, snow-slushy, empty street . . .
Tingle of frost in brow and feet . . .
Horse-breath goes dimly up like smoke.
No sound but the smacking stroke

Of a sergeant who flings each arm
Out and across to keep him warm,
And the sudden splashing crack
Of ice-pools broken by our track.

More dark houses, yet no sign
Of life . . . An axle's creak and whine . . .
The splash of hooves, the strain of trace . . .
Clatter: we cross the market place . . .

Deep quiet again, and on we lurch
Under the shadow of a church:
Its tower ascends, fog-wreathed and grim;
Within its aisles a light burns dim . . .

When, marvellous! from overhead,
Like abrupt speech of one deemed dead,
Speech-moved by some Superior Will,
A bell tolls thrice and then is still.

And suddenly I know that now
The priest within, with shining brow,
Lifts high the small round of the Host.
The server's tinkling bell is lost

In clash of the greater overhead.
Peace like a wave descends, is spread,
While watch the peasants' reverent eyes . . .
The bell's boom trembles, hangs, and dies.

O people who bow down to see
The Miracle of Calvary,
The bitter and the glorious,
Bow down, bow down and pray for us.

Once more our anguished way we take
Toward our Golgotha, to make
For all our lovers sacrifice.
Again the troubled bell tolls thrice.

And slowly, slowly, lifted up
Dazzles the overflowing cup.
O worshipping, fond multitude
Remember us too, and our blood.

Turn hearts to us as we go by,
Salute those about to die,
Plead for them, the deep bell toll:
Their sacrifice must soon be whole.

Entreat you for such hearts as break
With the premonitory ache
Of bodies, whose feet, hands, and side,
Must soon be torn, pierced, crucified.

Sue for them and all of us
Who the world over suffer thus,
Who have scarce time for prayer indeed,
Who only march and die and bleed.

.　　.　　.　　.

The town is left, the road leads on,
Bluely glaring in the sun,
Toward where in the sunrise gate
Death, honour, and fierce battle wait.

ROBERT NICHOLS

▶ The Life Style

Nobody interfered. My two uncles stood
close together in the midnight street and
punched each other until one of them
fell. On the edge of the crowd an aunt cried
and asked everyone to stop them, but nobody
interfered. They carried the one who had
fallen into the pub he'd left, and they
revived him with whisky and draught beer;
the other one walked away on the balls of
his feet. Always the family was like this—
at Christmas parties, Christenings and
similar occasions; it was, I suppose, the
Irish streak. On the other hand, it may
have been that, in that overheated kitchen
of my grandparents, I could find no love—
only envy and ingratitude. Often I am afraid:
most of the anger filtered through into
my parents' home, where I could find no
love. Now, in an overheated kitchen of my
own, I watch my wife and my own children.

EDWIN BROCK

The Rash Bride:
an Experience of the Mellstock Quire

We Christmas-carolled down the Vale, and up the Vale, and
round the Vale,
We played and sang that night as we were yearly wont to
do—
A carol in a minor key, a carol in the major D,
Then at each house: 'Good wishes: many Christmas joys to
you!'

Next, to the widow's John and I and all the rest drew on.
And I
Discerned that John could hardly hold the tongue of him
for joy.
The widow was a sweet young thing whom John was bent on
marrying,
And quiring at her casement seemed romantic to the boy.

'She'll make reply, I trust,' said he, 'to our salute? She
must!' said he,
'And then I will accost her gently—much to her surprise!—
For knowing not I am with you here, when I speak up and
call her dear
A tenderness will fill her voice, a bashfulness her eyes.'

So, by her window-square we stood; ay, with our lanterns
there we stood,
And he along with us,—not singing, waiting for a sign;
And when we'd quired her carols three a light was lit and
out looked she,
A shawl about her bedgown, and her colour red as wine.

And sweetly then she bowed her thanks, and smiled, and
spoke aloud her thanks;

When lo, behind her back there, in the room, a man
appeared.
I knew him—one from Woolcomb way—Giles Swetman—
honest as the day,
But eager, hasty; and I felt that some strange trouble
neared.

'How comes he there? . . . Suppose,' said we, 'she's wed of
late! Who knows?' said we.
—'She married yester-morning—only mother yet has
known
The secret o't!' shrilled one small boy. 'But now I've told,
let's wish 'em joy!'
A heavy fall aroused us: John had gone down like a stone.

We rushed to him and caught him round, and lifted him,
and brought him round,
When, hearing something wrong had happened, oped the
window she:
'Has one of you fallen ill?' she asked, 'by these night
labours overtasked?'
None answered. That she'd done poor John a cruel turn felt
we.

Till up spoke Michael: 'Fie, young dame! You've broke
your promise, sly young dame,
By forming this new tie, young dame, and jilting John so
true,
Who trudged to-night to sing to 'ee because he thought he'd
bring to 'ee
Good wishes as your coming spouse. May ye such trifling
rue!'

Her man had said no word at all; but being behind had
heard it all,

And now cried: 'Neighbours, on my soul I knew not 'twas
like this!'
And then to her: 'If I had known you'd had in tow not me
alone,
No wife should you have been of mine. It is a dear bought
bliss!'

She changed death-white, and heaved a cry: we'd never
heard so grieved a cry
As came from her at this from him: heartbroken quite
seemed she;
And suddenly, as we looked on, she turned, and rushed; and
she was gone,
Whither, her husband, following after, knew not; nor knew
we.

We searched till dawn about the house: within the house,
without the house,
We searched among the laurel boughs that grew beneath the
wall,
And then among the crocks and things, and stores for winter
junketings,
In linhay, loft, and dairy; but we found her not at all.

Then John rushed in: 'O friends,' he said, 'hear this, this,
this!' and bends his head:
'I've—searched round by the—*well*, and find the cover
open wide!
I am fearful that—I can't say what . . . Bring lanterns, and
some cords to knot.'
We did so, and we went and stood the deep dark hole beside.

And then they, ropes in hand, and I—ay, John, and all the
band, and I
Let down a lantern to the depths—some hundred feet and
more;

It glimmered like a fog-dimmed star; and there, beside its
    light, afar,
White drapery floated, and we knew the meaning that it bore.

The rest is naught . . . We buried her o' Sunday. Neigh-
    bours carried her;
And Swetman—he who'd married her—now miserablest of
    men,
Walked mourning first; and then walked John; just
    quivering, but composed anon;
And we the quire formed round the grave, as was the custom
    then.

Our old bass player, as I recall—his white hair blown—but
    why recall!—
His viol upstrapped, bent figure—doomed to follow her full
    soon—
Stood bowing, pale and tremulous; and next to him the rest
    of us . . .
We sang the Ninetieth Psalm to her—set to Saint Stephen's
    tune.

THOMAS HARDY

lhnhay: stable

▶ For Anne Gregory

'Never shall a young man,
Thrown into despair
By those great honey-coloured
Ramparts at your ear,
Love you for yourself alone
And not your yellow hair.'

'But I can get a hair-dye
And set such colour there,
Brown, or black, or carrot,
That young men in despair
May love me for myself alone
And not my yellow hair.'

'I heard an old religious man
But yesternight declare
That he had found a text to prove
That only God, my dear,
Could love you for yourself alone
And not your yellow hair.'

W. B. YEATS

▶ La Belle Dame Sans Merci

'O what can ail thee, knight-at-arms,
  Alone and palely loitering?
The sedge has wither'd from the lake,
And no birds sing.

'O what can ail thee, knight-at-arms,
  So haggard and so woe-begone?
The squirrel's granary is full,
  And the harvest's done.

'I see a lily on thy brow
  With anguish moist and fever dew,
And on thy cheeks a fading rose
  Fast withereth too.'

'I met a lady in the meads,
  Full beautiful—a faery's child,
Her hair was long, her foot was light,
  And her eyes were wild.

'I made a garland for her head,
  And bracelets too, and fragrant zone.
She look'd at me as she did love,
  And made sweet moan.

'I set her on my pacing steed
  And nothing else saw all day long,
For sidelong would she bend, and sing
  A faery's song.

'She found me roots of relish sweet,
  And honey wild and manna dew,
And sure in language strange she said
  "I love thee true."

'She took me to her elfin grot,
    And there she wept and sigh'd full sore,
And there I shut her wild wild eyes
    With kisses four.

'And there she lullèd me asleep,
    And there I dream'd—Ah! woe betide!
The latest dream I ever dream'd
    On the cold hill's side.

'I saw pale kings and princes too,
    Pale warriors, death-pale were they all:
They cried—"La belle Dame sans Merci
    Hath thee in thrall!"

'I saw their starved lips in the gloam
    With horrid warning gapèd wide,
And I awoke and found me here,
    On the cold hill's side.

'And this is why I sojourn here,
    Alone and palely loitering,
Though the sedge is wither'd from the lake
    And no birds sing.'

JOHN KEATS

zone: girdle

▶ Secret Police

They follow me, left right, left right.
   I look in windows to let them pass.
   The crowd pass, not they: if I turn,
They're out of sight, yet the blank eyes burn
Patient, reflected in the glass
For I am the man, the man they want to question.

Why watch, why wait, not arrest me now?
I may nod, perhaps, to the wrong man,
   Or ring, perhaps, at a certain house:
   Too nonchalant, or too much fuss,
A man with a plan, or too little plan,
The marked man, the man they want to question.

They follow me, left right, left right,
They watch me with unblinking eye.
   Till fear and creeping tiredness
   Confuse me, force me to confess
A yes to the thing I must deny,
Deny—deny—deny when the bland men question.

G. ROSTREVOR HAMILTON

▶ Spain, 1809

All day we had ridden through scarred, tawny hills.
  At last the cool
Of splashing water. Then two blackened mills,
  A slaughtered mule.

And there, crag-perched, the village—San Pedro—
  We came to burn.
(Two convoys ambushed in the gorge below.
  They had to learn.)

Not a sound. Not a soul. Not a goat left behind.
  They had been wise.
Those death's-head hovels watched us, bleared and blind,
  With holes for eyes.

Down the one street's foul gutter slowly crawled
  Like blood, dark-red,
The wine from goatskins, slashed and hacked, that sprawled
  Like human dead.

From a black heap, like some charred funeral-pyre,
  Curled up, forlorn,
Grey wisps of smoke, where they had fed the fire
  With their last corn.

What hatred in that stillness! Suddenly
  An infant's cry.
Child, mother, bedrid crone—we found the three,
  Too frail to fly.

We searched their very straw—one wineskin there.
  We grinned with thirst,
And yet?—that Spanish hate!—what man would dare
  To taste it first?

Below, our Captain called, 'Bring down the wench.'
  We brought her down—
Dark, brooding eyes that faced the smiling French
  With sullen frown.

'Señora, we are sent to burn the place.
  Your house I spare.'
Her proud chin nestled on her baby's face,
  Still silent there.

'Cold cheer you leave us!—one poor skin of wine!
  Before we sup,
You will honour us, Señora?' At his sign
  One filled a cup.

Calmly she took and, drinking, coldly smiled:
  We breathed more free.
But grimly our captain watched her—'Now your child.'
  Impassively,

She made the small mouth swallow. All was well.
  The street was fired.
And we, by that brave blaze, as twilight fell,
  Sat gaily tired,

Laughing and eating, while the wine went round,
  Carefree, until
A child's scream through the darkness. At the sound
  Our hearts stood still.

Dumbly we glanced in one another's eyes.
  Our thirst was dead.
And in its place once more that grim surmise
  Upreared its head.

One dragged her to the firelight. Ashen-grey,
    She hissed—'I knew
Not even the straw where an old woman lay
    Was safe from you.

'Now you are paid!' I never loved their wine,
    Had tasted none.
I will not tell, under that white moonshine,
    What things were done.

Twenty men mad with drink, and rage, and dread,
    Frenzied with pain—
That night the quiet millstream dribbled red
    With blood of Spain.

Under the moon across the gaunt sierra
    I fled alone.
Their balls whizzed wide. But in each tree lurked terror,
    In each stone.

Yes, men are brave. (Earth were a happier place,
    Were men less so.)
But I remember one pale woman's face
    In San Pedro.

F. L. LUCAS

▶ Apprenticed

'Come out and hear the waters shoot, the owlet hoot, the
    owlet hoot;
Yon crescent moon, a golden boat, hangs dim behind the
    tree, O!
The dropping thorn makes white the grass, O sweetest lass,
    and sweetest lass;
Come out and smell the ricks of hay adown the croft with
    me, O!'

'My granny nods before her wheel, and drops her reel, and
    drops her reel;
My father with his crony talks as gay as gay can be, O!
But all the milk is yet to skim, ere light wax dim, ere light
    wax dim;
How can I step adown the croft, my 'prentice lad, with thee,
    O?'

'And must ye bide, yet waiting's long, and love is strong,
    and love is strong;
And O, had I but served the time that takes so long to flee,
    O!
And thou, my lass, by morning light wast all in white, wast
    all in white,
And parson stood within the rails, a-marrying me and thee,
    O!'

JEAN INGELOW

▶ The Rime of the Ancient Mariner

PART I

It is an ancient Mariner,
And he stoppeth one of three.
'By thy long grey beard and glittering eye,
Now wherefore stopp'st thou me?

The Bridegroom's doors are opened wide,
And I am next of kin;
The guests are met, the feast is set:
May'st hear the merry din.'

He holds him with his skinny hand,
'There was a ship,' quoth he.
'Hold off! unhand me, grey-beard loon!'
Eftsoons his hand dropt he.

He holds him with his glittering eye—
The Wedding-Guest stood still,
And listens like a three years' child:
The Mariner hath his will.

The Wedding-Guest sat on a stone:
He cannot choose but hear;
And thus spake on that ancient man,
The bright-eyed Mariner.

'The ship was cheered, the harbour cleared,
Merrily did we drop
Below the kirk, below the hill,
Below the lighthouse top,

The Mariner tells
how the ship sailed
southward with a
good wind and fair
weather, till it
reached the Line.

The Sun came up upon the left,
Out of the sea came he!
And he shone bright, and on the right
Went down into the sea.

Higher and higher every day,
Till over the mast at noon—'
The Wedding-Guest here beat his breast,
For he heard the loud bassoon.

The Wedding-
Guest heareth
the bridal music;
but the Mariner
continueth his tale.

The bride hath paced into the hall,
Red as a rose is she;
Nodding their heads before her goes
The merry minstrelsy.

The Wedding-Guest he beat his breast,
Yet he cannot choose but hear;
And thus spake on that ancient man,
The bright-eyed Mariner.

The ship drawn by
a storm toward the
South Pole.

'And now the STORM-BLAST came, and he
Was tyrannous and strong:
He struck with his o'ertaking wings,
And chased us south along.

With sloping masts and dipping prow,
As who pursued with yell and blow
Still treads the shadow of his foe,
And forward bends his head,
The ship drove fast, loud roared the blast,
And southward aye we fled.

And now there came both mist and snow
And it grew wondrous cold:
And ice, mast-high, came floating by,
As green as emerald.

And through the drifts the snowy clifts
Did send a dismal sheen:
Nor shapes of men nor beasts we ken—
The ice was all between.

The ice was here, the ice was there,
The ice was all around:
It cracked and growled, and roared and howled,
Like noises in a swound!

At length did cross an Albatross,
Thorough the fog it came;
As if it had been a Christian soul,
We hailed it in God's name.

It ate the food it ne'er had eat,
And round and round it flew.
The ice did split with a thunder-fit;
The helmsman steered us through!

And a good south wind sprung up behind;
The Albatross did follow,
And every day, for food or play,
Came to the mariners' hollo!

In mist or cloud, on mast or shroud,
It perched for vespers nine;
Whiles all the night, through fog-smoke white
Glimmered the white moon-shine.'

'God save thee, ancient Mariner!
From the fiends, that plague thee thus!—
Why look'st thou so?'—'With my crossbow
I shot the ALBATROSS.

71

PART II

The Sun now rose upon the right:
Out of the sea came he,
Still hid in mist, and on the left
Went down into the sea.

And the good south wind still blew behind,
But no sweet bird did follow,
Nor any day for food or play
Came to the mariners' hollo!

His shipmates cry out against the ancient Mariner for killing the bird of good luck.

And I had done a hellish thing,
And it would work 'em woe:
For all averred I had killed the bird
That made the breeze to blow.
Ah wretch! said they, the bird to slay,
That made the breeze to blow!

But when the fog cleared off, they justify the same, and thus make themselves accomplices in the crime.

Nor dim nor red, like God's own head,
The glorious Sun uprist:
Then all averred I had killed the bird
That brought the fog and mist.
'Twas right, said they, such birds to slay,
That bring the fog and mist.

The fair breeze continues; the ship enters the Pacific Ocean, and sails northward, even till it reaches the Line.

The fair breeze blew, the white foam flew,
The furrow follow'd free;
We were the first that ever burst
Into that silent sea.

The ship hath been suddenly becalmed.

Down dropt the breeze, the sails dropt down,
'Twas sad as sad could be;
And we did speak only to break
The silence of the sea!

72

All in a hot and copper sky,
The bloody Sun, at noon,
Right up above the mast did stand,
No bigger than the Moon.

Day after day, day after day,
We stuck, nor breath nor motion;
As idle as a painted ship
Upon a painted ocean.

Water, water, every where,
And all the boards did shrink;
Water, water, every where,
Nor any drop to drink.

And the Albatross
begins to be
avenged.

The very deep did rot: O Christ!
That ever this should be!
Yea, slimy things did crawl with legs
Upon the slimy sea.

About, about, in reel and rout
The death-fires danced at night;
The water, like a witch's oils,
Burnt green, and blue, and white.

And some in dreams assured were
Of the Spirit that plagued us so;
Nine fathom deep he had followed us
From the land of mist and snow.

A spirit had
followed them: one
of the inhabitants of
this planet, neither
departed souls nor
angels; concerning
whom the learned
Jew, Josephus, and
the Platonic Con-
stantinopolitan,
Michael Psellus,
may be consulted.
They are very
numerous, and
there is no climate
or element without
one or more.

And every tongue, through utter drought,
Was withered at the root;
We could not speak, no more than if
We had been choked with soot.

The shipmates in their sore distress, would fain throw the whole guilt on the ancient Mariner: in sign whereof they hang the dead sea-bird round his neck.

Ah! well a-day! what evil looks
Had I from old and young!
Instead of the cross, the Albatross
About my neck was hung.

PART III

There passed a weary time. Each throat
Was parched, and glazed each eye.
A weary time! a weary time!
How glazed each weary eye,
The ancient Mariner beholdeth a sign in the element afar off.
When looking westward, I beheld
A something in the sky.

At first it seemed a little speck,
And then it seemed a mist;
It moved and moved, and took at last
A certain shape, I wist.

A speck, a mist, a shape, I wist!
And still it neared and neared:
As if it dodged a water-sprite,
It plunged, and tacked, and veered.

At its nearer approach, it seemeth him to be a ship; and at a dear ransom he freeth his speech from the bonds of thirst.
With throats unslaked, with black lips baked,
We could nor laugh nor wail;
Through utter drought all dumb we stood!
I bit my arm, I sucked the blood,
And cried, 'A sail! a sail!'

A flash of joy;
With throats unslaked, with black lips baked,
Agape they heard me call:
Gramercy! they for joy did grin,
And all at once their breath drew in,
As they were drinking all.

See! see! (I cried) she tacks no more!
Hither to work us weal;
Without a breeze, without a tide,
She steadies with upright keel!

And horror follows. For can it be a ship that comes onward without wind or tide?

The western wave was all a-flame,
The day was well nigh done!
Almost upon the western wave
Rested the broad bright Sun;
When that strange shape drove suddenly
Betwixt us and the Sun.

And straight the Sun was flecked with bars
(Heaven's Mother send us grace!)
As if through a dungeon-grate he peered
With broad and burning face.

It seemeth him but the skeleton of a ship.

Alas! (thought I, and my heart beat loud)
How fast she nears and nears!
Are those her sails that glance in the Sun,
Like restless gossameres?

Are those her ribs through which the Sun
Did peer, as through a grate?
And is that Woman all her crew?
Is that a DEATH? and are there two?
Is DEATH that Woman's mate?

And its ribs are seen as bars on the face of the setting Sun. The Spectre-Woman and her Death-mate, and no other, on board the skeleton ship.

Her lips were red, her looks were free,
Her locks were yellow as gold:
Her skin as white as leprosy,
The Night-mare LIFE-IN-DEATH was she,
Who thicks man's blood with cold.

Like vessel, like crew!

Death and Life-in-Death have diced for the ship's crew, and she (the latter) winneth the ancient Mariner.

The naked hulk alongside came,
And the twain were casting dice;
"The game is done! I've won! I've won!"
Quoth she, and whistles thrice.

No twilight within the courts of the Sun.

The Sun's rim dips; the stars rush out:
At one stride comes the dark;
With far-heard whisper, o'er the sea,
Off shot the spectre-bark.

At the rising of the Moon,

We listened and looked sideways up!
Fear at my heart, as at a cup,
My life-blood seem'd to sip!
The stars were dim, and thick the night,
The steersman's face by his lamp gleamed
        white;
From the sails the dew did drip—
Till clomb above the eastern bar
The hornèd Moon, with one bright star
Within the nether tip.

One after another.

One after one, by the star-dogged Moon,
Too quick for groan or sigh,
Each turned his face with a ghastly pang,
And cursed me with his eye.

His shipmates drop down dead.

Four times fifty living men
(And I heard nor sigh nor groan),
With heavy thump, a lifeless lump,
They dropped down one by one.

But Life-in-Death begins her work on the ancient Mariner

The souls did from their bodies fly,—
They fled to bliss or woe!
And every soul, it pass'd me by
Like the whizz of my crossbow!'

76

PART IV

'I fear thee, ancient Mariner!
I fear thy skinny hand!
And thou art long, and lank, and brown,
As is the ribbed sea-sand.

The Wedding-Guest feareth that a Spirit is talking to him.

I fear thee and thy glittering eye,
And thy skinny hand so brown.'—
'Fear not, fear not, thou Wedding-Guest!
This body dropt not down.

But the ancient Mariner assureth him of his bodily life, and proceedeth to relate his horrible penance.

Alone, alone, all, all alone,
Alone on a wide wide sea!
And never a saint took pity on
My soul in agony.

The many men, so beautiful!
And they all dead did lie:
And a thousand thousand slimy things
Lived on; and so did I.

He despiseth the creatures of the calm,

I looked upon the rotting sea,
And drew my eyes away;
I looked upon the rotting deck,
And there the dead men lay.

And envieth that *they* should live, and so many lie dead.

I looked to heaven, and tried to pray;
But or ever a prayer had gusht,
A wicked whisper came, and made
My heart as dry as dust.

I closed my lids, and kept them close,
And the balls like pulses beat;
For the sky and the sea, and the sea and the sky,
Lay like a load on my weary eye,
And the dead were at my feet.

But the curse
liveth for him
in the eye of the
dead men.

The cold sweat melted from their limbs,
Nor rot nor reek did they:
The look with which they looked on me
Had never passed away.

An orphan's curse would drag to hell
A spirit from on high;
But oh! more horrible than that
Is the curse in a dead man's eye!
Seven days, seven nights, I saw that curse,
And yet I could not die.

In his loneliness
and fixedness he
yearneth towards
the journeying
Moon, and the stars
that still sojourn,
yet still move
onward; and every-
where the blue sky
belongs to them,
and is their
appointed rest and
their native country
and their own
natural homes,
which they enter
unannounced, as
lords that are cert-
ainly expected, and
yet there is a silent
joy at their arrival.

The moving Moon went up the sky,
And no where did abide;
Softly she was going up,
And a star or two beside—

Her beams bemocked the sultry main,
Like April hoar-frost spread;
But where the ship's huge shadow lay,
The charmèd water burnt alway
A still and awful red.

By the light of the
Moon he beholdeth
God's creatures of
the great calm.

Beyond the shadow of the ship,
I watch'd the water-snakes:
They moved in tracks of shining white,
And when they rear'd, the elfish light
Fell off in hoary flakes.

Within the shadow of the ship
I watched their rich attire:
Blue, glossy green, and velvet black,
They coil'd and swam; and every track
Was a flash of golden fire.

78

O happy living things! no tongue
Their beauty might declare:
A spring of love gush'd from my heart,
And I blessed them unaware:
Sure my kind saint took pity on me,
And I blessed them unaware.

Their beauty
and their happiness.

He blesseth them
in his heart.

The self-same moment I could pray;
And from my neck so free
The Albatross fell off, and sank
Like lead into the sea.

The spell begins
to break.

PART V

O sleep! it is a gentle thing,
Beloved from pole to pole!
To Mary Queen the praise be given!
She sent the gentle sleep from Heaven,
That slid into my soul.

The silly buckets on the deck,
That had so long remained,
I dreamt that they were filled with dew;
And when I awoke, it rained.

By grace of the holy
Mother, the ancient
Mariner is refreshed
with rain.

My lips were wet, my throat was cold,
My garments all were dank;
Sure I had drunken in my dreams,
And still my body drank.

I moved, and could not feel my limbs:
I was so light—almost
I thought that I had died in sleep,
And was a blessed ghost.

He heareth sounds and seeth strange sights and commotions in the sky and the element.

And soon I heard a roaring wind:
It did not come anear;
But with its sound it shook the sails,
That were so thin and sere.

The upper air burst into life!
And a hundred fire-flags sheen,
To and fro they were hurried about!
And to and fro, and in and out,
The wan stars danced between.

And the coming wind did roar more loud,
And the sails did sigh like sedge;
And the rain poured down from one black cloud;
The Moon was at its edge.

The thick black cloud was cleft, and still
The Moon was at its side:
Like waters shot from some high crag,
The lightning fell with never a jag,
A river steep and wide.

The bodies of the ship's crew are inspired, and the ship moves on;

The loud wind never reached the ship,
Yet now the ship moved on!
Beneath the lightning and the Moon
The dead men gave a groan.

They groaned, they stirred, they all uprose,
Nor spake, nor moved their eyes:
It had been strange, even in a dream,
To have seen those dead men rise.

The helmsman steered, the ship moved on;
Yet never a breeze up-blew;
The mariners all 'gan work the ropes,
Where they were wont to do;
They raised their limbs like lifeless tools—
We were a ghastly crew.

The body of my brother's son
Stood by me, knee to knee:
The body and I pull'd at one rope,
But he said naught to me.'

'I fear thee, ancient Mariner!'
'Be calm, thou Wedding-Guest:
'Twas not those souls that fled in pain,
Which to their corses came again,
But a troop of spirits blest:

For when it dawned—they dropped their arms,
And clustered round the mast;
Sweet sounds rose slowly through their mouths,
And from their bodies passed.

Around, around, flew each sweet sound,
Then darted to the Sun;
Slowly the sounds came back again,
Now mixed, now one by one.

Sometimes a-dropping from the sky
I heard the sky-lark sing;
Sometimes all little birds that are,
How they seemed to fill the sea and air
With their sweet jargoning!

But not by the souls of the men, nor by demons of earth or middle air, but by a blessed troop of angelic spirits, sent down by the invocation of the guardian saint.

And now 'twas like all instruments,
Now like a lonely flute;
And now it is an angel's song,
That makes the heavens be mute.

It ceased; yet still the sails made on
A pleasant noise till noon,
A noise like of a hidden brook
In the leafy month of June,
That to the sleeping woods all night
Singeth a quiet tune.

Till noon we quietly sailed on,
Yet never a breeze did breathe:
Slowly and smoothly went the ship,
Moved onward from beneath.

The lonesome
Spirit from the
South Pole carries
on the ship as far as
the Line, in
obedience to the
angelic troop,
but still requireth
vengeance.

Under the keel nine fathom deep,
From the land of mist and snow,
The spirit slid: and it was he
That made the ship to go.
The sails at noon left off their tune,
And the ship stood still also.

The Sun, right up above the mast,
Had fixed her to the ocean:
But in a minute she 'gan stir,
With a short uneasy motion—
Backwards and forwards half her length
With a short uneasy motion.

Then like a pawing horse let go,
She made a sudden bound:
It flung the blood into my head,
And I fell down in a swound.

How long in that same fit I lay,
I have not to declare;
But ere my living life returned,
I heard, and in my soul discerned
Two voices in the air.

The Polar Spirit's
fellow-demons, the
invisible inhabitants
of the element, take
part in his wrong;
and two of them
relate, one to the
other, that penance
long and heavy
for the ancient
Mariner hath been
accorded to the
Polar Spirit,
who returneth
southward.

"Is it he?" quoth one, "Is this the man?
By him who died on cross,
With his cruel bow he laid full low
The harmless Albatross.

The spirit who bideth by himself
In the land of mist and snow,
He loved the bird that loved the man
Who shot him with his bow."

The other was a softer voice,
As soft as honey-dew:
Quoth he, "The man hath penance done,
And penance more will do."

PART VI

First Voice:
"But tell me, tell me! speak again,
Thy soft response renewing—
What makes that ship drive on so fast?
What is the ocean doing?"

Second Voice:
"Still as a slave before his lord,
The ocean hath no blast;
His great bright eye most silently
Up to the Moon is cast—

83

If he may know which way to go;
For she guides him smooth or grim.
See, brother, see! how graciously
She looketh down on him."

First Voice:

The Mariner hath been cast into a trance; for the angelic power causeth the vessel to drive northward faster than human life could endure.

"But why drives on that ship so fast,
Without or wave or wind?"

Second Voice:
"The air is cut away before,
And closes from behind.

Fly, brother, fly! more high, more high!
Or we shall be belated:
For slow and slow that ship will go,
When the Mariner's trance is abated."

The supernatural motion is retarded; the Mariner awakes, and his penance begins anew.

I woke, and we were sailing on
As in a gentle weather:
'Twas night, calm night, the moon was high;
The dead men stood together.

All stood together on the deck,
For a charnel-dungeon fitter:
All fixed on me their stony eyes,
That in the Moon did glitter.

The pang, the curse, with which they died,
Had never passed away:
I could not draw my eyes from theirs,
Nor turn them up to pray.

The curse is finally expiated.

And now this spell was snapt: once more
I viewed the ocean green,
And looked far forth, yet little saw
Of what had else been seen—

84

Like one, that on a lonesome road
Doth walk in fear and dread,
And having once turned round walks on,
And turns no more his head;
Because he knows, a frightful fiend
Doth close behind him tread.

But soon there breathed a wind on me,
Nor sound nor motion made:
Its path was not upon the sea,
In ripple or in shade.

It raised my hair, it fanned my cheek
Like a meadow-gale of spring—
It mingled strangely with my fears,
Yet it felt like a welcoming.

Swiftly, swiftly flew the ship,
Yet she sailed softly too:
Sweetly, sweetly blew the breeze—
On me alone it blew.

Oh! dream of joy! is this indeed
The lighthouse top I see?
Is this the hill? is this the kirk?
Is this mine own countree?

And the ancient
Mariner beholdeth
his native country.

We drifted o'er the harbour-bar,
And I with sobs did pray—
O let me be awake, my God!
Or let me sleep alway.

The harbour-bay was clear as glass,
So smoothly it was strewn!
And on the bay the moonlight lay,
And the shadow of the Moon.

The rock shone bright, the kirk no less
That stands above the rock:
The moonlight steeped in silentness
The steady weathercock.

And the bay was white with silent light,
Till rising from the same,
Full many shapes, that shadows were,
In crimson colours came.

A little distance from the prow
Those crimson shadows were:
I turned my eyes upon the deck—
Oh, Christ! what saw I there!

Each corse lay flat, lifeless and flat,
And, by the holy rood!
A man all light, a seraph-man,
On every corse there stood.

This seraph-band, each waved his hand:
It was a heavenly sight!
They stood as signals to the land,
Each one a lovely light;

This seraph-band, each waved his hand,
No voice did they impart—
No voice; but oh! the silence sank
Like music on my heart.

But soon I heard the dash of oars,
I heard the Pilot's cheer;
My head was turned perforce away,
And I saw a boat appear.

The Pilot and the Pilot's boy,
I heard them coming fast:
Dear Lord in Heaven! it was a joy
The dead men could not blast.

I saw a third—I heard his voice:
It is the Hermit good!
He singeth loud his godly hymns
That he makes in the wood.
He'll shrieve my soul, he'll wash away
The Albatross's blood.

PART VII

This hermit good lives in that wood   The Hermit of the
Which slopes down to the sea.   Wood.
How loudly his sweet voice he rears!
He loves to talk with marineres
That come from a far countree.

He kneels at morn, and noon, and eve—
He hath a cushion plump:
It is the moss that wholly hides
The rotted old oak-stump.

The skiff-boat neared: I heard them talk,
"Why, this is strange, I trow!
Where are those lights so many and fair,
That signal made but now?"

"Strange, by my faith!" the Hermit said—   Approacheth the
"And they answered not our cheer!   ship with wonder.
The planks look warped! and see those sails,
How thin they are and sere!
I never saw aught like to them,
Unless perchance it were

87

Brown skeletons of leaves that lag
My forest-brook along;
When the ivy-tod is heavy with snow,
And the owlet whoops to the wolf below,
That eats the she-wolf's young."

"Dear Lord! it hath a fiendish look"—
(The Pilot made reply)
"I am a-fear'd."—"Push on, push on!"
Said the Hermit cheerily.

The boat came closer to the ship,
But I nor spake nor stirred;
The boat came close beneath the ship,
And straight a sound was heard.

The ship
suddenly
sinketh.

Under the water it rumbled on,
Still louder and more dread:
It reached the ship, it split the bay;
The ship went down like lead.

The ancient
Mariner is saved
in the Pilot's boat.

Stunned by that loud and dreadful sound,
Which sky and ocean smote,
Like one that hath been seven days drowned
My body lay afloat;
But swift as dreams, myself I found
Within the Pilot's boat.

Upon the whirl, where sank the ship,
The boat spun round and round;
And all was still, save that the hill
Was telling of the sound.

I moved my lips—the Pilot shrieked
And fell down in a fit;
The holy Hermit raised his eyes,
And prayed where he did sit.

88

I took the oars: the Pilot's boy,
Who now doth crazy go,
Laughed loud and long, and all the while
His eyes went to and fro.
"Ha! ha!" quoth he, "full plain I see
The Devil knows how to row."

And now, all in my own countree,
I stood on the firm land!
The Hermit stepp'd forth from the boat,
And scarcely he could stand.

"O shrieve me, shrieve me, holy man!"
The Hermit crossed his brow.
"Say quick," quoth he, "I bid thee say—
What manner of man art thou?"

The ancient Mariner earnestly entreateth the Hermit to shrieve him; and the penance of life falls on him.

Forthwith this frame of mine was wrenched
With a woful agony,
Which forced me to begin my tale;
And then it left me free.

Since then, at an uncertain hour,
That agony returns:
And till my ghastly tale is told,
This heart within me burns.

And ever and anon throughout his future life an agony constraineth him to travel from land to land;

I pass, like night, from land to land;
I have strange power of speech;
That moment that his face I see,
I know the man that must hear me:
To him my tale I teach.

What loud uproar bursts from that door!
The wedding-guests are there:
But in the garden-bower the bride
And bride-maids singing are:
And hark the little vesper bell,
Which biddeth me to prayer!

O Wedding-Guest! this soul hath been
Alone on a wide wide sea:
So lonely 'twas, that God Himself
Scarce seemèd there to be.

O sweeter than the marriage-feast,
'Tis sweeter far to me,
To walk together to the kirk
With a goodly company!—

To walk together to the kirk,
And all together pray,
While each to his great Father bends,
Old men, and babes, and loving friends,
And youths and maidens gay!

Farewell, farewell! but this I tell
To thee, thou Wedding-Guest!
He prayeth well, who loveth well
Both man and bird and beast.

He prayeth best, who loveth best
All things both great and small;
For the dear God who loveth us,
He made and loveth all.'

The Mariner, whose eye is bright,
Whose beard with age is hoar,
Is gone: and now the Wedding-Guest
Turned from the bridegroom's door.

He went like one that hath been stunned,
And is of sense forlorn:
A sadder and a wiser man
He rose the morrow morn.

SAMUEL TAYLOR COLERIDGE

▶ Wild Sports of the West

The landlord's coat is tulip red,
A beacon on the wine-dark moor;
He turns his well-bred foreign devil's face,
While his bailiff trots before.

His furious hooves drum fire from stone,
A beautiful sight when gone;
Contemplation holds the noble horseman
In his high mould of bone.

Not so beautiful the bandy bailiff,
Churlish servant of an alien will:
Behind the hedge a maddened peasant
Poises his shotgun for the kill.

Evening brings the huntsman home,
Blood of pheasants in a bag:
Beside a turfrick the cackling peasant
Cleanses his ancient weapon with a rag.

The fox, evicted from a thicket,
Evades with grace the snuffling hounds:
But a transplanted bailiff, in a feudal paradise,
Patrols for God His private grounds.

JOHN MONTAGUE

▶ View of a Pig

The pig lay on a barrow dead.
It weighed, they said, as much as three men.
Its eyes closed, pink white eyelashes.
Its trotters stuck straight out.

Such weight and thick pink bulk
Set in death seemed not just dead.
It was less than lifeless, further off.
It was like a sack of wheat.

I thumped it without feeling remorse.
One feels guilty insulting the dead,
Walking on graves. But this pig
Did not seem able to accuse.

It was too dead. Just so much
A poundage of lard and pork.
Its last dignity had entirely gone.
It was not a figure of fun.

Too dead now to pity.
To remember its life, din, stronghold
Of earthly pleasure as it had been,
Seemed a false effort, and off the point.

Too deadly factual. Its weight
Oppressed me—how could it be moved?
And the trouble of cutting it up!
The gash in its throat was shocking, but not pathetic.

Once I ran at a fair in the noise
To catch a greased piglet
That was faster and nimbler than a cat,
Its squeal was the rending of metal.

Pigs must have hot blood, they feel like ovens.
Their bite is worse than a horse's—
They chop a half-moon clean out.
They eat cinders, dead cats.

Distinctions and admirations such
As this one was long finished with.
I stared at it a long time. They were going to scald it,
Scald it and scour it like a doorstep.

TED HUGHES

▶ Neighbour

This neighbour-soldier found his death
in a delayed Flanders, with no sound
of shouting, bugles, gun-fire.

After forty years nursing a proud wound
he died in a suburban house
rarely called on by friends or relations.

Rising to reveille, he fell (we think)
and gashed his head upon the grate.
There was no witness, no trooper's comforting.

Lying stiff and bloody in his no-man's-land
he did not hear the milkman slam the gate,
the postman shove a gas-bill through the door.

Police came, and cousins, and the old man
was carted away like a couch, with no ceremony.
Since then the room's had many visitors.

EDWARD STOREY

▶ Earthquake

An old man's flamingo-coloured kite
Twitched higher over tiled roofs.
Idly gazing through the metal gauze
That nets the winter sun beyond my sliding windows,
I notice that all the telegraph-poles along the lane
Are waggling convulsively, and the wires
Bounce like skipping-ropes round flustered birds.
The earth creeps under the floor. A cherry tree
Agitates itself outside, but it is no wind
That makes the long bamboo palisade
Begin to undulate down all its length.

The clock stammers and stops. There is a queer racket,
Like someone rapping on the wooden walls,
Then through the ceiling's falling flakes I see
The brass handles on a high chest of drawers
Dithering and dancing in a brisk distraction.
The lamp swings like a headache, and the whole house
Rotates slightly on grinding rollers.
Smoothly, like a spoilt child putting out a tongue,
A drawer shoots half-out, and quietly glides back again,
Closed with a snap of teeth, a sharper click
Than such a casual grimace prepared me for.

The stove-pipe's awkward elbow
Twangles its three supporting wires. Doors
Slam, fly open: my quiet maid erupts from
Nowhere, blushing furiously, yet smiling wildly
As if to explain, excuse, console and warn.
Together, like lost children in a fairy-tale
Who escape from an enchanter's evil cottage,
We rush out into the slightly unbalanced garden. A pole
Vibrates still like a plucked bass string,
But the ground no longer squirms beneath our feet,
And the trees are composing themselves, have birds again.

In the spooky quiet, a 'plane drones
Like a metal top, and though the sound
Gives a sense of disaster averted,
And is even oddly re-assuring, as
The pulse of confident engines,
Throbbing high above an electric storm, can comfort,
We feel that somewhere out of sight
Something has done its worst. Meanwhile,
The house tries to look as if nothing had happened,
And over the roof's subtle curves
Lets the flamingo-coloured kite fly undisturbed.

JAMES KIRKUP

▶ In Memoriam

The flowers left thick at nightfall in the wood
This Eastertide call into mind the men,
Now far from home, who, with their sweethearts, should
Have gathered them and will do never again.

EDWARD THOMAS

▶ I Know Where I'm Going

I know where I'm going,
I know who's going with me,
I know who I love,
But the dear knows who I'll marry.

I'll have stockings of silk
Shoes of fine green leather,
Combs to buckle my hair
And a ring for every finger.

Feather beds are soft,
Painted rooms are bonny;
But I'd leave them all
To go with my love Johnny.

Some say he's dark,
I say he's bonny,
He's the flower of them all
My handsome, winsome Johnny.

I know where I'm going,
I know who's going with me,
I know who I love,
But the dear knows who I'll marry.

ANON.

The young man in this ballad is a soldier.

▶ Snake

A snake came to my water-trough
On a hot, hot day, and I in pyjamas for the heat,
To drink there.

In the deep, strange-scented shade of the great dark carob-
tree
I came down the steps with my pitcher
And must wait, must stand and wait, for there he was at the
trough before me.

He reached down from a fissure in the earth-wall in the
gloom
And trailed his yellow-brown slackness soft-bellied down,
over the edge of the stone trough
And rested his throat upon the stone bottom,
And where the water had dripped from the tap, in a small
clearness,
He sipped with his straight mouth,
Softly drank through his straight gums, into his slack long
body,
Silently.

Someone was before me at my water-trough,
And I, like a second comer, waiting.

He lifted his head from his drinking, as cattle do,
And looked at me vaguely, as drinking cattle do,
And flickered his two-forked tongue from his lips, and mused
a moment,
And stooped and drank a little more,
Being earth-brown, earth-golden from the burning bowels
of the earth,
On the day of Sicilian July, with Etna smoking.

The voice of my education said to me
He must be killed,
For in Sicily the black, black snakes are innocent, the gold
are venomous.

And voices in me said, If you were a man
You would take a stick and break him now, and finish him
off.

But I must confess how I liked him,
How glad I was he had come like a guest in quiet, to drink
at my water-trough
And depart peaceful, pacified, and thankless,
Into the burning bowels of this earth.

Was it cowardice, that I dared not kill him?
Was it perversity, that I longed to talk to him?
Was it humility to feel so honoured?
I felt so honoured.

And yet those voices:
'*If you were not afraid, you would kill him!*'

And truly I was afraid, I was most afraid,
But even so, honoured still more
That he should seek my hospitality
From out the dark door of the secret earth.

He drank enough
And lifted his head, dreamily, as one who has drunken,
And flicked his tongue like a forked night on the air, so
black,
Seeming to lick his lips,
And looked around like a god, unseeing, into the air,
And slowly turned his head,
And slowly, very slowly, as if thrice adream,

Proceeded to draw his slow length curving round
And climb again the broken bank of my wall-face.

And as he put his head into that dreadful hole,
And as he slowly drew up, snake-easing his shoulders, and
  entered farther,
A sort of horror, a sort of protest against his withdrawing
  into that horrid black hole,
Deliberately going into the blackness, and slowly drawing
  himself after,
Overcame me now his back was turned.

I looked round, I put down my pitcher,
I picked up a clumsy log
And threw it at the water-trough with a clatter.

I think it did not hit him,
But suddenly that part of him that was left behind con-
  vulsed in undignified haste,
Writhed like lightning, and was gone
Into the black hole, the earth-lipped fissure in the wall-
  front,
At which, in the intense still noon, I stared with fascination.

And immediately I regretted it.
I thought how paltry, how vulgar, what a mean act!
I despised myself and the voices of my accursed human
  education.

And I thought of the albatross,
And I wished he would come back, my snake.

For he seemed to me again like a king,
Like a king in exile, uncrowned in the underworld,
Now due to be crowned again.

And so, I missed my chance with one of the lords
Of life.
And I have something to expiate;
A pettiness.

D. H. LAWRENCE

▶ Mia Carlotta

Guiseppe, da barber, ees greata for 'mash',
He gotta da bigga, da blacka mustache,
Good clo'es an' good styla an' playnta good cash.

W'enevera Guiseppe ees walk on da street,
Da people dey talka, 'How nobby! how neat!
How softa da handa, how smalla da feet.'

He raisa hees hat an' he shaka hees curls,
An' smila weeth teetha so shiny like pearls;
O! many da heart of da seelly young girls
   He gotta.
  Yes, playnta he gotta—
   But notta
   Carlotta!

Guiseppe, da barber, he maka da eye,
An' lika de steam engine puffa an' sigh,
For catcha Carlotta w'en she ees go by.

Carlotta she walka weeth nose in da air,
An' look through Guiseppe weeth far-away stare,
As eef she no see dere ees som'body dere.

Guiseppe, da barber, he gotta da cash,
He gotta da clo'es an' da bigga mustache,
He gotta da seelly young girls for 'da mash',
   But notta—
  You bat my life, notta—
   Carlotta,
   I gotta!

T. A. DALY

▶ The Lady of Shalott

PART I

On either side the river lie
Long fields of barley and of rye,
That clothe the wold and meet the sky;
And thro' the field the road runs by
     To many-tower'd Camelot;
And up and down the people go,
Gazing where the lilies blow
Round an island there below,
     The island of Shalott.

Willows whiten, aspens quiver,
Little breezes dusk and shiver
Thro' the wave that runs for ever
By the island in the river
     Flowing down to Camelot.
Four grey walls, and four grey towers,
Overlook a space of flowers,
And the silent isle imbowers
     The Lady of Shalott.

By the margin, willow-veil'd,
Slide the heavy barges trail'd
By slow horses; and unhail'd
The shallop flitteth silken-sail'd
     Skimming down to Camelot:
But who hath seen her wave her hand?
Or at the casement seen her stand?
Or is she known in all the land,
     The Lady of Shalott?

Only reapers, reaping early
In among the bearded barley,
Hear a song that echoes cheerly
From the river winding clearly,
      Down to tower'd Camelot:
And by the moon the reaper weary,
Piling sheaves in uplands airy,
Listening, whispers,, 'Tis the fairy
      Lady of Shalott.'

PART II

There she weaves by night and day
A magic web with colours gay.
She has heard a whisper say,
A curse is on her if she stay
      To look down to Camelot.
She knows not what the curse may be,
And so she weaveth steadily,
And little other care hath she,
      The Lady of Shalott.

And moving thro' a mirror clear
That hangs before her all the year,
Shadows of the world appear.
There she sees the highway near
      Winding down to Camelot:
There the river eddy whirls,
And there the surly village-churls,
And the red cloaks of market girls,
      Pass onward from Shalott.

Sometimes a troop of damsels glad,
An abbot on an ambling pad,
Sometimes a curly shepherd-lad,
Or long-hair'd page in crimson clad,

Goes by to tower'd Camelot;
And sometimes thro' the mirror blue
The knights come riding two and two:
She hath no loyal knight and true,
     The Lady of Shalott.

But in her web she still delights
To weave the mirror's magic sights,
For often thro' the silent nights
A funeral, with plumes and lights
     And music, went to Camelot:
Or when the moon was overhead,
Came two young lovers lately wed;
'I am half sick of shadows,' said
     The Lady of Shalott.

PART III

A bow-shot from her bower-eaves,
He rode between the barley-sheaves,
The sun came dazzling thro' the leaves,
And flamed upon the brazen greaves
     Of bold Sir Lancelot.
A red-cross knight for ever kneel'd
To a lady in his shield,
That sparkled on the yellow field,
     Beside remote Shalott.

The gemmy bridle glitter'd free,
Like to some branch of stars we see
Hung in the golden Galaxy.
The bridle bells rang merrily
     As he rode down to Camelot:
And from his blazon'd baldric slung
A mighty silver bugle hung,
And as he rode his armour rung
     Beside remote Shalott.

All in the blue unclouded weather
Thick-jewell'd shone the saddle-leather,
The helmet and the helmet-feather
Burn'd like one burning flame together,
  As he rode down to Camelot.
As often thro' the purple night,
Below the starry clusters bright,
Some bearded meteor, trailing light,
Moves over still Shalott.

His broad clear brow in sunlight glow'd;
On burnish'd hooves his war-horse trode;
From underneath his helmet flow'd
His coal-black curls as on he rode,
As he rode down to Camelot.
From the bank and from the river
He flash'd into the crystal mirror,
'Tirra lirra,' by the river
  Sang Sir Lancelot.

She left the web, she left the loom,
She made three paces thro' the room,
She saw the water-lily bloom,
She saw the helmet and the plume,
  She look'd down to Camelot.
Out flew the web and floated wide;
The mirror crack'd from side to side;
'The curse is come upon me,' cried
  The Lady of Shalott.

PART IV

In the stormy east-wind straining,
The pale yellow woods were waning,
The broad stream in his banks complaining,
Heavily the low sky raining

Over tower'd Camelot;
Down she came and found a boat
Beneath a willow left afloat,
And round about the prow she wrote
The Lady of Shalott.

And down the river's dim expanse
Like some bold seer in a trance,
Seeing all his own mischance—
With a glassy countenance
Did she look to Camelot.
And at the closing of the day
She loosed the chain, and down she lay;
The broad stream bore her far away,
The Lady of Shalott.

Lying, robed in snowy white
That loosely flew to left and right—
The leaves upon her falling light—
Thro' the noises of the night
She floated down to Camelot:
And as the boat-head wound along
The willowy hills and fields among,
They heard her singing her last song,
The Lady of Shalott.

Heard a carol, mournful, holy,
Chanted loudly, chanted lowly,
Till her blood was frozen slowly,
And her eyes were darken'd wholly
Turn'd to tower'd Camelot.
For ere she reach'd upon the tide
The first house by the water-side,
Singing in her song she died,
The Lady of Shalott.

Under tower and balcony,
By garden-wall and gallery,
A gleaming shape she floated by,
Dead-pale between the houses high,
    Silent into Camelot.
Out upon the wharfs they came,
Knight and burgher, lord and dame,
And round the prow they read her name,
    The Lady of Shalott.

Who is this? and what is here?
And in the lighted palace near
Died the sound of royal cheer;
And they cross'd themselves for fear,
    All the knights at Camelot:
But Lancelot mused a little space;
He said, 'She has a lovely face;
God in his mercy lend her grace,
    The Lady of Shalott.'

ALFRED, LORD TENNYSON

▶ Incendiary

That one small boy with a face like pallid cheese
And burnt-out little eyes could make a blaze
As brazen, fierce and huge, as red and gold
And zany yellow as the one that spoiled
Three thousand guineas' worth of property
And crops at Godwin's Farm on Saturday
Is frightening, as fact and metaphor:
An ordinary match intended for
The lighting of a pipe or kitchen fire
Misused may set a whole menagerie
Of flame-fanged tigers roaring hungrily.
And frightening, too, that one small boy should set
The sky on fire and choke the stars to heat
Such skinny limbs and such a little heart
Which would have been content with one warm kiss,
Had there been anyone to offer this.

VERNON SCANNELL

▶ Romantic Suicide

He was not wicked, merely wrong,
Always wrong whatever he did,
And when he fell in love the song
He sang was pitched too high and loud
Offending those white ears he loved.
And when she went he bravely hid
His grief and walked into the water,
For that was what the poems he read
Said was the appropriate thing
To do if you had lost your lover.
He did not know the world of rhyme
Has laws outside the world of time
And what is beautiful in verse
May well outside be anything
But beautiful, indeed far worse
Than images whose conscious aim
It is to sicken and alarm.
And so he sank into the lake
And wallowed with the perch and pike
Among green wavering scenery.
Seven days were lost before they hauled
His corpse from lecherous weeds and mud,
And we who gathered there to see
That romantic suicide
Saw a fat inflated blubber,
A thing composed of greyish rubber.
His face we will not dwell upon
Through creatures in the waters had
No such pretty scruples there.
Enough to say we turned away,
And what pity might have touched
Our hearts was swamped by nausea.

All we could do was dumbly pray
That God prove less fastidious:
Extend his mercy, sweet and strong,
To one not wicked, merely wrong.

VERNON SCANNELL

▶ The Young Labourers

Hanmer, midwinter; twenty degrees of frost;
And round the small spa with its conical hill
Ranking shoulder to shoulder in a warlock host

The pine plantations, steep, gloomy and still.
We labourers in the nursery in the rimy morning
Stamped and beat hands and strove for tasks to fill

Two laggard hours until the sun returning
Cleared the high skyline and began to thaw
The locked earth. Then we were soon scorning

Gauntlets and mufflers, and merry in the raw
Mountainous air, tackled the seedling pines.
But first they had to be made easy to draw,

So one going ahead, with a fork's tines
Loosened the roots; and following with bent backs,
Straddling the toy trees in their orderly lines,

We bundled them in twenty-fives with a strip of flax
—For a moment my hands can almost remember the knot . . .
And next, clod-footed, aproned in sacks,

We stirred the puddling-tub until we got
A thin porridge of mud, and dipping the roots
Bundle by bundle, heeled them back in the plot

Ready for the planter-gang. We soft recruits
Tramped home aching in the starry dark,
Lit the stove in our shack, took off our boots,

Stuffed our bellies and pipes and forgot the work
In bawdry, till someone suggested a swim—
And eagerly we clattered out. In the little park

The baths lay moonlit, sulphurous, agleam,
Smoking in the icy air. A quick strip—
Nobody shivered long on the bath's brim—

It was naked into the pungent waters, leap!
Swim lapped in warmth, clamber out bellowing,
Towel lustily and race back home to sleep
Quickly and deep for the day's labour following.

ARTHUR WOLSELEY RUSSELL

Hanmer: a hot springs resort in New Zealand
warlock: goblin

▶ Pied Beauty

Glory be to God for dappled things—
For skies of couple-colour as a brindled cow;
For rose-moles all in stipple upon trout that swim;
Fresh-firecoal chestnut-falls; finches' wings;
Landscape plotted and pieced—fold, fallow, and plough;
And all trades, their gear and tackle and trim.

All things counter, original, spare, strange;
Whatever is fickle, freckled (who knows how?)
With swift, slow; sweet, sour; adazzle, dim;
He fathers-forth whose beauty is past change:
Praise Him.

GERARD MANLEY HOPKINS

▶ The Green Bushes

As I was a-walking one morning in May
To hear the birds whistle and see lambkins play,
I spied a young damsel, so softly sang she,
Down by the green bushes where she chanced to meet me.

'Oh why are you loitering here, pretty maid?'
'I am waiting for my true love', then softly she said.
'Shall I be your sweetheart, and will you agree
To leave your true love and follow with me?

'I'll give you fine beavers and fine silken gowns;
I'll give you fine petticoats flounced to the ground;
I'll buy you rich jewels and live but for thee,
If you'll leave your true love and follow with me.'

'I want none of your beavers or fine silken hose,
For I'm not so poor as to marry for clothes,
But if you'll be constant and true unto me,
I'll leave my true love and follow with thee.

'Now let us be going, fine sir, if you please,
Oh let us be going from under these trees,
For yonder is coming my true love, I see,
Down by the green bushes where he thinks to meet me.'

And when he came there, and found she had gone,
He sighed very deeply, he sighed all alone:
'She has gone with another, and forsaken me,
So farewell, ye green bushes, where she vowed to meet me.'

ANON.

▶ The Wife of Usher's Well

There lived a wife at Usher's Well,
And a wealthy wife was she;
She had three stout and stalwart sons,
And sent them o'er the sea.

They hadna been a week from her,
A week but barely ane,
When word came to the carline wife
That her three sons were gane.

They hadna been a week from her,
A week but barely three,
When word came to the carline wife
That her sons she'd never see.

'I wish the wind may never cease,
Nor fashes in the flood,
Till my three sons come hame to me
In earthly flesh and blood!'

It fell about the Martinmas,
When nights are lang and mirk,
The carline wife's three sons came hame,
And their hats were o' the birk.

It neither grew in dyke nor ditch,
Nor yet in ony sheugh,
But at the gates o' Paradise
That birk grew fair eneugh.

carline wife: old woman
fashes: troubles
mirk: dark
birk: made of birch-bark
sheugh: furrow

'Blow up the fire, my maidens!
Bring water from the well!
For all my house shall feast this night,
Since my three sons are well.'

And she has made to them a bed,
She's made it large and wide;
And she's ta'en her mantle her about,
Sat down at the bedside.

Then up and crew the red, red cock,
And up and crew the grey;
The eldest to the youngest said,
''Tis time we were away.'

The cock he hadna craw'd but ance,
And clapp'd his wings at a',
When the youngest to the eldest said,
'Brother, we must awa'.

'The cock doth craw, the day doth daw,
The channerin' worm doth chide;
Gin we be miss'd out o' our place,
A sair pain we must bide.'

'Lie still, lie still but a little wee while,
Lie still but if we may;
Gin my mother should miss us when she
    wakes,
She'll go mad ere it be day.'

daw: dawn
channerin': complaining
gin: if

'Fare ye weel, my mother dear!
Fareweel to barn and byre!
And fare ye weel, the bonny lass
That kindles my mother's fire!'

ANON.

The woman and her sons were members of the witch cult. The
birch tree is traditionally associated with witchcraft. She laid a
curse that the sea be lashed by winds if her sons did not come
home. The sons were dead, but their spirits came to her from
Avalon, the Celtic Paradise where birch trees grew in profusion.

▶ A Mountain Stream, Kalaw, Burma

We climbed from the burning plain
Strangers in a strange land
The jungle holding its terrors
The black panther straddling the road

Eyes burning in pitch
Ready to spring
Faint rustle of leaves
Betraying the hidden cobra

We climbed from the burning plain
Red skins chafed with the sweat
And dust of a day on the plain.

And a cold moon
Unveiled her beauty above us;
We halted in a clearing
Where a stream rushed under a culvert
Across the road

Faint emerald light
Glistened on a moist
And moss-grown rock

Then came to our ears
Noise as of water falling
From the woods high above
Falling in pools, misting the night air
With infinitesimal cloud-spray

Glad now in heart we built a fire
By the roadside
Collecting dry sticks and leaves

And then descended
And against the General's strictest orders
Drank from the natural water
Risking whatever disease

We were only once disturbed further that night
By the pounding of hooves
And the dull beat of something against a tree

It was a water-buffalo
Chained to a mighty teak-tree
Banging great horns on the bark
In the first cold grey of the dawn.

PETER RUSSELL

▶ African Beggar

Sprawled in the dust outside the Syrian store,
a target for small children, dogs and flies,
a heap of verminous rags and matted hair,
he watches us with cunning, reptile eyes,
his noseless, smallpoxed face creased in a sneer.

Sometimes he shows his yellow stumps of teeth
and whines for alms, perceiving that we bear
the curse of pity; a grotesque mask of death,
with hands like claws about his begging-bowl.

But often he is lying all alone
within the shadow of a crumbling wall,
lost in the trackless jungle of his pain,
clutching the pitiless red earth in vain
and whimpering like a stricken animal.

RAYMOND TONG

▶ Ozymandias

I met a traveller from an antique land
Who said: 'Two vast and trunkless legs of stone
Stand in the desert. Near them on the sand,
Half sunk, a shattered visage lies, whose frown
And wrinkled lip and sneer of cold command
Tell that its sculptor well those passions read
Which yet survive, stamped on these lifeless things,
The hand that mocked them and the heart that fed.
And on the pedestal these words appear:
"My name is Ozymandias, king of kings:
Look on my works, ye mighty, and despair!"
Nothing beside remains. Round the decay
Of that colossal wreck, boundless and bare,
The lone and level sands stretch far away.'

PERCY BYSSHE SHELLEY

▶ The Collier

When I was born on Amman hill
A dark bird crossed the sun.
Sharp on the floor the shadow fell;
I was the youngest son.

And when I went to the County School
I worked in a shaft of light.
In the wood of the desk I cut my name:
Dai for Dynamite.

The tall black hills my brothers stood;
Their lessons all were done.
From the door of the school when I ran out
They frowned to watch me run.

The slow grey bells they rung a chime
Surly with grief or age.
Clever or clumsy, lad or lout,
All would look for a wage.

I learnt the valley flowers' names
And the rough bark knew my knees.
I brought home trout from the river
And spotted eggs from the trees.

A coloured coat I was given to wear
Where the lights of the rough land shone.
Still jealous of my favour
The tall black hills looked on.

They dipped my coat in the blood of a kid
And they cast me down a pit,
And although I crossed with strangers
There was no way up from it.

Soon as I went from the County School
I worked in a shaft. Said Jim,
'You will get your chain of gold, my lad,
But not for a likely time.'

And one said, 'Jack was not raised up
When the wind blew out the light
Though he interpreted their dreams
And guessed their fears by night.'

And Tom, he shivered his leper's lamp
For the stain that round him grew;
And I heard mouths pray in the after-damp
When the picks would not break through.

They changed words there in darkness
And still through my head they run,
And white on my limbs is the linen sheet
And gold on my neck the sun.

VERNON WATKINS

More than one interpretation is possible here. The story of Joseph,
for instance, stands behind the poem. The poet himself has said
that he sees the collier as recovering in hospital.

▶ Autobiographical Note

Beeston, the place, near Nottingham:
We lived there for three years or so.
Each Saturday at two-o'clock
We queued up for the matinee,
All the kids for streets around
With snotty noses, giant caps,
Cut down coats and heavy boots,
The natural enemies of cops
And schoolteachers. Profane and hoarse
We scrambled, yelled and fought until
The Picture Palace opened up
And we, like Hamelin children, forced
Our bony way into the hall.
That much is easy to recall;
Also the reek of chewing-gum,
Gob-stoppers and liquorice,
But of the flickering myths themselves
Not much remains. The hero was
A milky wide-brimmed hat, a shape
Astride the arched white stallion;
The villain's horse and hat were black.
Disbelief did not exist
And laundered virtue always won
With quicker gun and harder fist,
And all of us applauded it.
Yet I remember moments when
In solitude I'd find myself
Brooding on the sooty man,
The bristling villain, who could move
Imagination in a way
The well-shaved hero never could,
And even warm the nervous heart
With something oddly close to love.

VERNON SCANNELL

▶ A Private

This ploughman dead in battle slept out of doors
Many a frozen night, and merrily
Answered staid drinkers, good bedmen, and all bores:
'At Mrs. Greenland's Hawthorn Bush,' said he,
'I slept.' None knew which bush. Above the town,
Beyond 'The Drover,' a hundred spot the down
In Wiltshire. And where now at last he sleeps
More sound in France—that, too, he secret keeps.

EDWARD THOMAS

▶ The Host of the Air

O'Driscoll drove with a song
The wild duck and the drake,
From the tall and tufted weeds
Of the drear Hart Lake.

And he saw how the weeds grew dark
At the coming of night tide;—
And he dreamed of the long dim hair,
Of Bridget his bride.

He heard while he sang and dreamed
A piper piping away,
And never was piping so sad,
And never was piper so gay.

And he saw young men and young girls
Who danced on a level place,
And Bridget his bride among them,
With a sad and a gay face.

The dancers crowded about him,
And many a sweet thing said;
And a young man brought him red wine,
And a young girl white bread.

But Bridget drew him by the sleeve,
Away from the merry bands,
To old men playing at cards,
With a twinkle of ancient hands.

The bread and wine had a doom;
For these were the host of the air;
He sat and played in a dream
Of her long dim hair.

He played with the merry old men,
And thought not of evil chance,
Till one bore Bridget his bride
Away from the merry dance.

He bore her away in his arms,
The handsomest young man there;
And his neck and his breast and his arms
Were drowned in her long dim hair.

O'Driscoll got up from the grass
And scattered the cards with a cry;
But the old men and dancers were gone
As a cloud faded into the sky.

He knew now the host of the air,
And his heart was blackened by dread;
And he ran to the door of his house:
Old women were keening the dead.

But he heard high up in the air
A piper piping away;
And never was piping so sad,
And never was piping so gay.

W. B. YEATS

▶ 'The General Elliott'

He fell in victory's fierce pursuit,
Holed through and through with shot;
A sabre sweep had hacked him deep
'Twixt neck and shoulder-knot.

The potman cannot well recall,
The ostler never knew,
Whether that day was Malplaquet,
The Boyne, or Waterloo.

But there he hangs, a tavern sign,
With foolish bold regard
For cock and hen and loitering men
And wagons down the yard.

Raised high above the hayseed world
He smokes his china pipe;
And now surveys the orchard ways,
The damsons clustering ripe—

Stares at the churchyard slabs beyond,
Where country neighbours lie:
Their brief renown set lowly down,
But his invades the sky.

He grips a tankard of brown ale
That spills a generous foam:
Often he drinks, they say, and winks
At drunk men lurching home.

No upstart hero may usurp
That honoured swinging seat;
His seasons pass with pipe and glass
Until the tale's complete—

And paint shall keep his buttons bright
Though all the world's forgot
Whether he died for England's pride
By battle or by pot.

ROBERT GRAVES

▶ Journey of the Magi

'A cold coming we had of it,
Just the worst time of the year
For a journey, and such a long journey:
The ways deep and the weather sharp,
The very dead of winter.'
And the camels galled, sore-footed, refractory,
Lying down in the melting snow.
There were times we regretted
The summer palaces on slopes, the terraces,
And the silken girls bringing sherbet.
Then the camel men cursing and grumbling
And running away, and wanting their liquor and women,
And the night-fires going out, and the lack of shelters,
And the cities hostile and the towns unfriendly
And the villages dirty and charging high prices:
A hard time we had of it.
At the end we preferred to travel all night,
Sleeping in snatches,
With the voices singing in our ears, saying
That this was all folly.

Then at dawn we came down to a temperate valley,
Wet, below the snow line, smelling of vegetation;
With a running stream and a water-mill beating the darkness,
And three trees on the low sky,
And an old white horse galloped away in the meadow.
Then we came to a tavern with vine-leaves over the lintel,
Six hands at an open door dicing for pieces of silver,
And feet kicking the empty wine-skins.
But there was no information, and so we continued
And arrived at evening, not a moment too soon
Finding the place; it was (you may say) satisfactory.

All this was a long time ago, I remember,
And I would do it again, but set down
This set down
This: were we led all that way for
Birth or Death? There was a Birth, certainly,
We had evidence and no doubt. I had seen birth and death,
But had thought they were different; this Birth was
Hard and bitter agony for us, like Death, our death.
We returned to our places, these Kingdoms,
But no longer at ease here, in the old dispensation,
With an alien people clutching their gods.
I should be glad of another death.

T. S. ELIOT

▶ Light

The night has a thousand eyes,
And the day but one;
Yet the light of the bright world dies
With the dying sun.

The mind has a thousand eyes,
And the heart but one;
Yet the light of a whole life dies
When love is done.

F. W. BOURDILLON

▶ Incident in Hyde Park, 1803

The impulses of April, the rain-gems, the rose-cloud,
The frilling of flowers in the westering love-wind!
And here through the Park come gentlemen riding,
And there through the Park come gentlemen riding,
And behind the glossy horses Newfoundland dogs follow.
Says one dog to the other, "This park, sir, is mine, sir".
The reply is not wanting; hoarse clashing and mouthing
Arouses the masters.
Then Colonel Montgomery, of the Life Guards, dismounts.
   'Whose dog is this?' The reply is not wanting,
From Captain Macnamara, Royal Navy: 'My dog.'
   'Then call your dog off, or by God he'll go sprawling.'
   'If my dog goes sprawling, you must knock me down after.'
   'Your name?' 'Macnamara, and yours is—'
   'Montgomery.'
   'And why, sir, not call your dog off?' 'Sir, I chose
Not to do so, no man has dictated to me yet,
And you, I propose, will not change that.' 'This place,
For adjusting disputes, is not proper'—and the Colonel,
Back to the saddle, continues, 'If your dog
Fights my dog, I warn you, I knock your dog down.
For the rest, you are welcome to know where to find me,
Colonel Montgomery; and you will of course
Respond with the due information.' 'Be sure of it'.

Now comes the evening, green-twinkling, clear-echoing,
And out to Chalk-farm the Colonel, the Captain,
Each with his group of believers, have driven.
   Primrose Hill on an April evening
   Even now in a fevered London
   Sings a vesper sweet; but these
   Will try another music. Hark!
These are the pistols; let us test them; quite perfect.
Montgomery, Macnamara six paces, two faces;

Montgomery, Macnamara—both speaking together
In nitre and lead, the style is incisive,
Montgomery fallen, Macnamara half-falling,
The surgeon exploring the work of the evening—
And the Newfoundland dogs stretched at home in the fire-
   light.

The coroner's inquest; the view of one body;
And then, pale, supported, appears at Old Bailey
James Macnamara, to whom this arraignment:
   You stand charged
   That you
   With force and arms
   Did assault Robert Montgomery,
   With a certain pistol
   Of the value of ten shillings,
Loaded with powder and a leaden bullet
Which the gunpowder, feloniously exploded,
Drove into the body of Robert Montgomery,
   And gave
   One mortal wound;
Thus you did kill and slay
The said Robert Montgomery.
O heavy imputation! O dead that yet speaks!
O evening transparency, burst to red thunder!

Speak, Macnamara. He, tremulous as a windflower,
   Exactly imparts what had slaughtered the Colonel.
   'Insignificant the origin of the fact now before you;
Defending our dogs, we grew warm; that was nature;
That heat of itself had not led to disaster.
From defence to defiance was the leap that destroyed.
At once he would have at my deity, Honour—
   If you are offended you know where to find me.
On one side, I saw the wide mouths of Contempt,
Mouth to mouth working, a thousand vile gunmouths;
I am a Captain in the British Navy.'

Then said Lord Hood: 'For Captain Macnamara,
He is a gentleman and so says the Navy.'
Then said Lord Nelson: 'I have known Macnamara
Nine years, a gentleman, beloved in the Navy,
Not to be affronted by any man, true,
Yet as I stand here before God and my country,
Macnamara has never offended, and would not,
Man, woman, child.' Then a spring-tide of admirals,
Almost Neptune in person, proclaim Macnamara
Mild, amiable, cautious, as any in the Navy;
And Mr Garrow rises, to state that if need be,
To assert the even temper and peace of his client,
He would call half the Captains in the British Navy.

Now we are shut from the duel that Honour
Must fight with the Law; no eye can perceive
The fields wherein hundreds of shadowy combats
Must decide between a ghost and a living idolon—
A ghost with his army of the terrors of bloodshed,
A half-ghost with the grand fleet of names that like sunrise
Have dazzled the race with their march on the ocean.

Twenty minutes. How say you?

> Not guilty.

Then from his chair with his surgeon the Captain
Walks home to his dog, his friends' acclamations
Supplying some colour to the pale looks he had,
Less pale than Montgomery's; and Honour rides on.

EDMUND BLUNDEN

idolon: idea

▶ Isabella; or, The Pot of Basil

A Story from Boccaccio

Fair Isabel, poor simple Isabel!
   Lorenzo, a young palmer in Love's eye!
They could not in the self-same mansion dwell
   Without some stir of heart, some malady;
They could not sit at meals but feel how well
   It soothèd each to be the other by;
They could not, sure, beneath the same roof sleep
But to each other dream, and nightly weep.

With every morn their love grew tenderer,
   With every eve deeper and tenderer still;
He might not in house, field, or garden stir,
   But her full shape would all his seeing fill;
And his continual voice was pleasanter
   To her, than noise of trees or hidden rill;
Her lute-string gave an echo of his name,
She spoilt her half-done broidery with the same.

He knew whose gentle hand was at the latch,
   Before the door had given her to his eyes;
And from her chamber-window he would catch
   Her beauty farther than the falcon spies;
And constant as her vespers would he watch,
   Because her face was turn'd to the same skies;
And with sick longing all the night outwear,
To hear her morning-step upon the stair.

A whole long month of May in this sad plight
   Made their cheeks paler by the break of June:
'To-morrow will I bow to my delight,
   To-morrow will I ask my lady's boon.'—

'O may I never see another night,
    Lorenzo, if thy lips breathe not love's tune.'—
So spake they to their pillows; but, alas,
Honeyless days and days did he let pass;

Until sweet Isabella's untouch'd cheek
    Fell sick within the rose's just domain,
Fell thin as a young mother's, who doth seek
    By every lull to cool her infant's pain:
'How ill she is,' said he, 'I may not speak,
    And yet I will, and tell my love all plain:
If looks speak love-laws, I will drink her tears,
And at the least 'twill startle off her cares.'

So said he one fair morning, and all day
    His heart beat awfully against his side;
And to his heart he inwardly did pray
    For power to speak; but still the ruddy tide
Stifled his voice, and puls'd resolve away—
    Fever'd his high conceit of such a bride,
Yet brought him to the meekness of a child:
Alas! when passion is both meek and wild!

So once more he had wak'd and anguishèd
    A dreary night of love and misery,
If Isabel's quick eye had not been wed
    To every symbol on his forehead high;
She saw it waxing very pale and dead,
    And straight all flush'd; so, lispèd tenderly
'Lorenzo!'—here she ceas'd her timid quest,
But in her tone and look he read the rest.

'O Isabella, I can half perceive
    That I may speak my grief into thine ear;
If thou didst ever anything believe,
    Believe how I love thee, believe how near

My soul is to its doom: I would not grieve
    Thy hand by unwelcome pressing, would not fear
Thine eyes by gazing; but I cannot live
Another night, and not my passion shrive.

'Love! thou art leading me from wintry cold,
    Lady! thou leadest me to summer clime,
And I must taste the blossoms that unfold
    In its ripe warmth this gracious morning time.'
So said, his erewhile timid lips grew bold,
    And poesied with hers in dewy rhyme:
Great bliss was with them, and great happiness
Grew, like a lusty flower in June's caress.

Parting they seem'd to tread upon the air,
    Twin roses by the zephyr blown apart
Only to meet again more close, and share
    The inward fragrance of each other's heart.
She, to her chamber gone, a ditty fair
    Sang, of delicious love and honey'd dart;
He with light steps went up a western hill,
And bade the sun farewell, and joy'd his fill.

All close they met again, before the dusk
    Had taken from the stars its pleasant veil,
All close they met, all eves, before the dusk
    Had taken from the stars its pleasant veil,
Close in a bower of hyacinth and musk,
    Unknown of any, free from whispering tale.
Ah! better had it been for ever so,
Than idle ears should pleasure in their woe.

       ·   ·   ·   ·   ·

With her two brothers this fair lady dwelt,
    Enrichèd from ancestral merchandize,

And for them many a weary hand did swelt
   In torchèd mines and noisy factories,
And many once proud-quiver'd loins did melt
   In blood from stinging whip;—with hollow eyes
Many all day in dazzling river stood,
To take the rich-ored driftings of the flood.

For them the Ceylon diver held his breath,
   And went all naked to the hungry shark;
For them his ears gush'd blood; for them in death
   The seal on the cold ice with piteous bark
Lay full of darts; for them alone did seethe
   A thousand men in troubles wide and dark;
Half ignorant, they turn'd an easy wheel,
That set sharp racks at work, to pinch and peel.

.   .   .   .   .

These brethren having found by many signs
   What love Lorenzo for their sister had,
And how she lov'd him too, each unconfines
   His bitter thoughts to other, well nigh mad
That he, the servant of their trade designs,
   Should in their sister's love be blithe and glad,
When 'twas their plan to coax her by degrees
To some high noble and his olive-trees.

And many a jealous conference had they,
   And many times they bit their lips alone,
Before they fix'd upon a surest way
   To make the youngster for his crime atone;
And at the last, these men of cruel clay
   Cut Mercy with a sharp knife to the bone;
For they resolvèd in some forest dim
To kill Lorenzo, and there bury him.

So on a pleasant morning, as he leant
   Into the sun-rise, o'er the balustrade
Of the garden-terrace, towards him they bent
   Their footing through the dews; and to him said,
'You seem there in the quiet of content,
   Lorenzo, and we are most loth to invade
Calm speculation; but if you are wise,
Bestride your steed while cold is in the skies.

'Today we purpose, aye, this hour we mount
   To spur three leagues towards the Apennine;
Come down, we pray thee, ere the hot sun count
   His dewy rosary on the eglantine'.
Lorenzo, courteously as he was wont,
   Bow'd a fair greeting to these serpents' whine;
And went in haste, to get in readiness,
With belt, and spur, and bracing huntsman's dress.

And as he to the court-yard pass'd along,
   Each third step did he pause, and listen'd oft
If he could hear his lady's matin-song,
   Or the light whisper of her footstep soft;
And as he thus over his passion hung,
   He heard a laugh full musical aloft;
When, looking up, he saw her features bright
Smile through an in-door lattice, all delight.

'Love, Isabel!' said he, 'I was in pain
   Lest I should miss to bid thee a good morrow:
Ah! what if I should lose thee, when so fain
   I am to stifle all the heavy sorrow
Of a poor three hours' absence? but we'll gain
   Out of the amorous dark what day doth borrow.
Good bye! I'll soon be back.'—'Good bye!' said she—
And as he went she chanted merrily.

So the two brothers and their murder'd man
    Rode past fair Florence, to where Arno's stream
Gurgles through straiten'd banks, and still doth fan
    Itself with dancing bulrush, and the bream
Keeps head against the freshets. Sick and wan
    The brothers' faces in the ford did seem,
Lorenzo's flush with love.—They pass'd the water
Into a forest quiet for the slaughter.

There was Lorenzo slain and buried in,
    There in that forest did his great love cease;
Ah! when a soul doth thus its freedom win,
    It aches in loneliness—is ill at peace
As the break-covert blood-hounds of such sin:
    They dipp'd their swords in the water, and did tease
Their horses homeward, with convulsèd spur,
Each richer by his being a murderer.

They told their sister how, with sudden speed,
    Lorenzo had ta'en ship for foreign lands,
Because of some great urgency and need
    In their affairs, requiring trusty hands.
Poor Girl! put on thy stifling widow's weed,
    And 'scape at once from Hope's accursed bands;
Today thou wilt not see him, nor tomorrow,
And the next day will be a day of sorrow.

She weeps alone for pleasures not to be;
    Sorely she wept until the night came on,
And then, instead of love, O misery!
    She brooded o'er the luxury alone:
His image in the dusk she seem'd to see,
    And to the silence made a gentle moan,
Spreading her perfect arms upon the air,
And on her couch low murmuring 'Where? O where?'

· ·· · · ·

In the mid days of autumn, on their eves
    The breath of Winter comes from far away,
And the sick west continually bereaves
    Of some gold tinge, and plays a roundelay
Of death among the bushes and the leaves,
    To make all bare before he dares to stray
From his north cavern. So sweet Isabel
By gradual decay from beauty fell,

Because Lorenzo came not. Oftentimes
    She ask'd her brothers, with an eye all pale,
Striving to be itself, what dungeon climes
    Could keep him off so long? They spake a tale
Time after time, to quiet her. Their crimes
    Came on them, like a smoke from Hinnom's vale;
And every night in dreams they groan'd aloud,
To see their sister in her snowy shroud.

And she had died in drowsy ignorance,
    But for a thing more deadly dark than all;
It came like a fierce potion, drunk by chance,
    Which saves a sick man from the feather'd pall
For some few gasping moments; like a lance,
    Waking an Indian from his cloudy hall
With cruel pierce, and bringing him again
Sense of the gnawing fire at heart and brain.

It was a vision.—In the drowsy gloom,
    The dull of midnight, at her couch's foot
Lorenzo stood, and wept: the forest tomb
    Had marr'd his glossy hair which once could shoot
Lustre into the sun, and put cold doom
    Upon his lips, and taken the soft lute
From his lorn voice, and past his loamèd ears
Had made a miry channel for his tears.

Strange sound it was, when the pale shadow spake;
  For there was striving, in its piteous tongue,   ·
To speak as when on earth it was awake,
  And Isabella on its music hung:
Languor there was in it, and tremulous shake,
  As in a palsied Druid's harp unstrung;
And through it moan'd a ghostly under-song,
Like hoarse night-gusts sepulchral briars among.

Its eyes, though wild, were still all dewy bright
  With love, and kept all phantom fear aloof
From the poor girl by magic of their light,
  The while it did unthread the horrid woof
Of the late darken'd time,—the murderous spite
  Of pride and avarice,—the dark pine roof
In the forest,—and the sodden turfed dell,
Where, without any word, from stabs he fell.

Saying moreover, 'Isabel, my sweet!
  Red whortle-berries droop above my head,
And a large flint-stone weighs upon my feet;
  Around me beeches and high chestnuts shed
Their leaves and prickly nuts; a sheep-fold bleat
  Comes from beyond the river to my bed:
Go, shed one tear upon my heather-bloom,
And it shall comfort me within the tomb.

'I am a shadow now, alas! alas!
  Upon the skirts of human-nature dwelling
Alone: I chant alone the holy mass,
  While little sounds of life are round me knelling,
And glossy bees at noon do fieldward pass,
  And many a chapel bell the hour is telling,
Paining me through: those sounds grow strange to me,
And thou art distant in Humanity.

'I know what was, I feel full well what is,
   And I should rage, if spirits could go mad;
Though I forget the taste of earthly bliss,
   That paleness warms my grave, as though I had
A Seraph chosen from the bright abyss
   To be my spouse: thy paleness makes me glad;
Thy beauty grows upon me, and I feel
A greater love through all my essence steal.'

The Spirit mourn'd 'Adieu!'—dissolv'd and left
   The atom darkness in a slow turmoil;
As when of healthful midnight sleep bereft,
   Thinking on rugged hours and fruitless toil,
We put our eyes into a pillowy cleft,
   And see the spangly gloom froth up and boil:
It made sad Isabella's eyelids ache,
And in the dawn she started up awake;

'Ha! ha!' said she, 'I knew not this hard life,
   I thought the worst was simple misery;
I thought some Fate with pleasure or with strife
   Portion'd us—happy days, or else to die;
But there is crime—a brother's bloody knife!
   Sweet Spirit, thou hast school'd my infancy:
I'll visit thee for this, and kiss thine eyes,
And greet thee morn and even in the skies.'

When the full morning came, she had devised
   How she might secret to the forest hie;
How she might find the clay, so dearly prized,
   And sing to it one latest lullaby;
How her short absence might be unsurmised,
   While she the inmost of the dream would try.
Resolv'd, she took with her an aged nurse,
And went into that dismal forest-hearse.

See, as they creep along the river side,
   How she doth whisper to that aged Dame,
And, after looking round the champaign wide,
   Shows her a knife.—'What feverous hectic flame
Burns in thee, child?—What good can thee betide,
   That thou should'st smile again?'—The evening came,
And they had found Lorenzo's earthy bed;
The flint was there, the berries at his head.

Who hath not loiter'd in a green churchyard,
   And let his spirit, like a demon-mole,
Work through the clayey soil and gravel hard,
   To see skull, coffin'd bones, and funeral stole;
Pitying each form that hungry Death hath marr'd,
   And filling it once more with human soul?
Ah! this is holiday to what was felt
When Isabella by Lorenzo knelt.

She gaz'd into the fresh-thrown mould, as though
   One glance did fully all its secrets tell;
Clearly she saw, as other eyes would know
   Pale limbs at bottom of a crystal well;
Upon the murderous spot she seem'd to grow,
   Like to a native lily of the dell:
Then with her knife, all sudden, she began
To dig more fervently than misers can.

Soon she turn'd up a soiled glove, whereon
   Her silk had play'd in purple phantasies,
She kiss'd it with a lip more chill than stone,
   And put it in her bosom, where it dries
And freezes utterly unto the bone
   Those dainties made to still an infant's cries:
Then 'gan she work again; nor stay'd her care,
But to throw back at times her veiling hair.

That old nurse stood beside her wondering,
　　Until her heart felt pity to the core
At sight of such a dismal labouring,
　　And so she kneeled, with her locks all hoar,
And put her lean hands to the horrid thing:
　　Three hours they labour'd at this travail sore;
At last they felt the kernel of the grave,
And Isabella did not stamp and rave.

　　　　　　·　·　·　·　·

With duller steel than the Persean sword
　　They cut away no formless monster's head,
But one, whose gentleness did well accord
　　With death, as life. The ancient harps have said
Love never dies, but lives, immortal Lord:
　　If Love impersonate was ever dead,
Pale Isabella kiss'd it, and low moan'd.
'Twas love; cold,—dead indeed, but not dethroned.

In anxious secrecy they took it home,
　　And then the prize was all for Isabel:
She calm'd its wild hair with a golden comb,
　　And all around each eye's sepulchral cell
Pointed each fringed lash; the smeared loam
　　With tears, as chilly as a dripping well,
She drench'd away:—and still she comb'd, and kept
Sighing all day—and still she kiss'd, and wept.

Then in a silken scarf,—sweet with the dews
Of precious flowers pluck'd in Araby,
And divine liquids come with odorous ooze
　　Through the cold serpent-pipe refreshfully,—
She wrapp'd it up; and for its tomb did choose
　　A garden-pot, wherein she laid it by,
And cover'd it with mould, and o'er it set
Sweet Basil, which her tears kept ever wet.

And she forgot the stars, the moon, and sun,
　　And she forgot the blue above the trees,
And she forgot the dells where waters run,
　　And she forgot the chilly autumn breeze;
She had no knowledge when the day was done,
　　And the new morn she saw not: but in peace
Hung over her sweet Basil evermore,
And moisten'd it with tears unto the core.

And so she ever fed it with thin tears,
　　Whence thick, and green, and beautiful it grew,
So that it smelt more balmy than its peers
　　Of Basil-tufts in Florence; for it drew
Nurture besides, and life, from human fears,
　　From the fast mouldering head there shut from view:
So that the jewel, safely casketed,
Came forth and in perfumed leafits spread.

　　　.　　.　　.　　.　　.

O leave the palm to wither by itself;
　　Let not quick Winter chill its dying hour!—
It may not be—those Baalites of pelf,
　　Her brethren, noted the continual shower
From her dead eyes; and many a curious elf,
　　Among her kindred, wonder'd that such dower
Of youth and beauty should be thrown aside
By one mark'd out to be a Noble's bride.

And, furthermore, her brethren wonder'd much
　　Why she sat drooping by the Basil green,
And why it flourish'd as by magic touch;
　　Greatly they wonder'd what the thing might mean:
They could not surely give belief, that such
　　A very nothing would have power to wean
Her from her own fair youth, and pleasures gay,
And even remembrance of her love's delay.

Therefore they watch'd a time when they might sift
   This hidden whim; and long they watch'd in vain;
For seldom did she go to chapel-shrift,
   And seldom felt she any hunger-pain;
And when she left, she hurried back, as swift
   As bird on wing to breast its eggs again;
And, patient as a hen-bird, sat her there
Beside her Basil, weeping through her hair.

Yet they contriv'd to steal the Basil-pot,
   And to examine it in secret place;
The thing was vile with green and livid spot,
   And yet they knew it was Lorenzo's face:
The guerdon of their murder they had got,
   And so left Florence in a moment's space,
Never to turn again—Away they went,
With blood upon their heads, to banishment.

O Melancholy, turn thine eyes away!
   O Music, Music, breathe despondingly!
O Echo, Echo, on some other day,
   From isles Lethean, sigh to us—O sigh!
Spirits of grief, sing not your 'Well-a-way!'
   For Isabel, sweet Isabel, will die;
Will die a death too lone and incomplete,
Now they have ta'en away her Basil sweet.

Piteous she look'd on dead and senseless things,
   Asking for her lost Basil amorously;
And with melodious chuckle in the strings
   Of her lorn voice, she oftentimes would cry
After the Pilgrim in his wanderings,
   To ask him where her Basil was; and why
'Twas hid from her: 'For cruel 'tis,' said she,
'To steal my Basil-pot away from me.'

And so she pined, and so she died forlorn,
　　Imploring for her Basil to the last.
No heart was there in Florence but did mourn
　　In pity of her love, so overcast.
And a sad ditty of this story born
　　From mouth to mouth through all the country pass'd:
Still is the burthen sung—'O cruelty,
To steal my Basil-pot away from me!'

JOHN KEATS

Hinnom's vale: where Ahaz, King of Israel, following heathen
　practice burnt his children in the fire (Chronicles 11, 28, iii).
Persean sword: Perseus' sword, with which he cut off the
　gorgon Medusa's head.
Baalites of pelf: worshippers of money

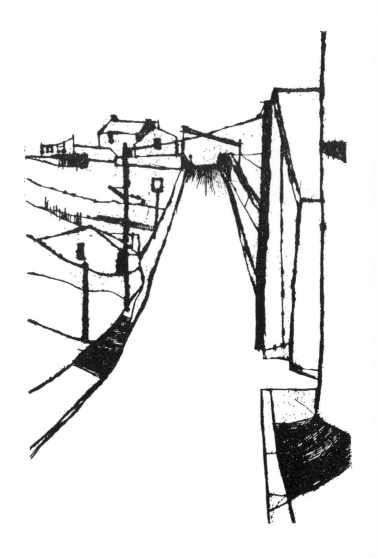

▶ My Luve's like a Red, Red Rose

O, my luve's like a red, red rose,
That's newly sprung in June:
O, my luve's like the melodie
That's sweetly played in tune.

As fair art thou, my bonnie lass,
So deep in luve am I;
And I will luve thee still, my dear,
Till a' the seas gang dry.

Till a' the seas gang dry, my dear,
And the rocks melt wi' the sun;
I will luve thee still, my dear,
While the sands o' life shall run.

And fare thee weel, my only luve!
And fare thee weel a while!
And I will come again, my luve,
Tho' it were ten thousand mile.

ROBERT BURNS

▶ A Subaltern's Love-Song

Miss J. Hunter Dunn, Miss J. Hunter Dunn,
Furnish'd and burnished by Aldershot sun,
What strenuous singles we played after tea,
We in the tournament—you against me.

Love-thirty, love-forty, oh, weakness of joy,
The speed of a swallow, the grace of a boy,
With carefullest carelessness, gaily you won,
I am weak from your loveliness, Joan Hunter Dunn.

Miss Joan Hunter Dunn, Miss Joan Hunter Dunn,
How mad I am, sad I am, glad that you won.
The warm-handled racket is back in its press,
But my shock-headed victor, she loves me no less.

Her father's euonymus shines as we walk,
And swing past the summer-house, buried in talk,
And cool the verandah that welcomes us in
To the six-o'clock news and a lime-juice and gin.

The scent of the conifers, sound of the bath,
The view from my bedroom of moss-dappled path,
As I struggle with double-end evening tie,
For we dance at the Golf Club, my victor and I.

On the floor of her bedroom lie blazer and shorts
And the cream-coloured walls are be-trophied with sports,
And westering, questioning settles the sun
On your low-leaded window, Miss Joan Hunter Dunn.

The Hillman is waiting, the light's in the hall,
The pictures of Egypt are bright on the wall,
My sweet, I am standing beside the oak stair
And there on the landing's the light on your hair.

By roads 'not adopted', by woodlanded ways,
She drove to the club in the late summer haze,
Into nine-o'clock Camberley, heavy with bells
And mushroomy, pine-woody, evergreen smells.

Miss Joan Hunter Dunn, Miss Joan Hunter Dunn,
I can hear from the car-park the dance has begun.
Oh! full Surrey twilight! importunate band!
Oh! strongly adorable tennis-girl's hand!

Around us are Rovers and Austins afar,
Above us, the intimate roof of the car,
And here on my right is the girl of my choice,
With the tilt of her nose and the chime of her voice,

And the scent of her wrap, and the words never said,
And the ominous, ominous dancing ahead.
We sat in the car park till twenty to one
And now I'm engaged to Miss Joan Hunter Dunn.

JOHN BETJEMAN

euonymus: a shrub

▶ Felix Randal

Felix Randal the farrier, O he is dead then? my duty all
    ended,
Who have watched his mould of man, big-boned and hardy-
    handsome
Pining, pining, till time when reason rambled in it and some
Fatal four disorders, fleshed there, all contended?

Sickness broke him. Impatient he cursed at first, but mended
Being anointed and all; though a heavenlier heart began
    some
Months earlier, since I had our sweet reprieve and ransom
Tendered to him. Ah well, God rest him all road ever he
    offended!

This seeing the sick endears them to us, us too it endears.
My tongue had taught thee comfort, touch had quenched
    thy tears,
Thy tears that touched my heart, child, Felix, poor Felix
    Randal;

How far from then forethought of, all thy more boisterous
    years,
When thou at the random grim forge, powerful amidst
    peers,
Didst fettle for the great grey drayhorse his bright and
    battering sandal!

GERARD MANLEY HOPKINS

farrier: blacksmith
sweet reprieve and ransom: Holy Communion
all road ever: in whatever way
random: crudely built
fettle: make ready

▶ The Trap

The first night that the monster lurched
Out of the forest on all fours,
He saw its shadow in his dream
Circle the house, as though it searched
For one it loved or hated. Claws
On gravel and a rabbit's scream
Ripped the fabric of his dream.

Waking between dark and dawn
And sodden sheets, his reason quelled
The shadow and the nightmare sound.
The second night it crossed the lawn
A brute voice in the darkness yelled.
He struggled up, woke raving, found
His wall-flowers trampled to the ground.

When rook wings beckoned the shadows back
He took his rifle down, and stood
All night against the leaded glass.
The moon ticked round. He saw the black
Elm-skeletons in the doomsday-wood,
The sailing and the failing stars
And red coals dropping between bars.

The third night such a putrid breath
Fouled, flared his nostrils, that he turned,
Turned, but could not lift, his head.
A coverlet as thick as death
Oppressed him: he crawled out: discerned
Across the door his watchdog, dead.
'Build a trap', the neighbours said.

All that day he built his trap
With metal jaws and a spring as thick
As the neck of a man. One touch
Triggered the hanging teeth: jump, snap,
And lightning guillotined the stick
Thrust in its throat. With gun and torch
He set his engine in the porch.

The fourth night in their beds appalled
His neighbours heard the hunting roar
Mount, mount to an exultant shriek.
At daybreak timidly they called
His name, climbed through the splintered door,
And found him sprawling in the wreck,
Naked with a severed neck.

JON STALLWORTHY

▶ The Rear-guard

Groping along the tunnel, step by step,
He winked his prying torch with patching glare
From side to side and sniffed the unwholesome air.

Tins, boxes, bottles, shapes too vague to know,
A mirror smashed, the mattress from a bed;
And he, exploring fifty feet below
The rosy gloom of battle overhead.
Tripping, he grabbed the wall; saw someone lie
Humped at his feet, half-hidden by a rug,
And stopped to give the sleeper's arm a tug.
'I'm looking for headquarters'. No reply.
'God blast your neck' (For days he'd had no sleep.)
'Get up and guide me through this stinking place.'

Savage, he kicked a soft, unanswering heap,
And flashed his beam across the livid face
Terribly glaring up, whose eyes yet wore
Agony dying hard ten days before;
And fists of fingers clutched a blackening wound.
Alone he staggered on until he found
Dawn's ghost that filtered down a shafted stair
To the dazed, muttering creatures underground
Who hear the boom of shells in muffled sound.
At last, with sweat of horror in his hair,
He climbed through darkness to the twilight air,
Unloading hell behind him step by step.

SIEGFRIED SASSOON

▶ My Last Duchess

That's my last Duchess painted on the wall,
Looking as if she were alive; I call
That piece a wonder, now: Fra Pandolf's hands
Worked busily a day, and there she stands.
Will 't please you sit and look at her? I said
'Fra Pandolf' by design, for never read
Strangers like you that pictured countenance,
The depth and passion of its earnest glance,
But to myself they turned (since none puts by
The curtain I have drawn for you, but I)
And seemed as they would ask me, if they durst,
How such a glance came there; so, not the first
Are you to turn and ask thus. Sir, 'twas not
Her husband's presence only, called that spot
Of joy into the Duchess' cheek: perhaps
Fra Pandolf chanced to say 'Her mantle laps
Over my Lady's wrist too much', or 'Paint
Must never hope to reproduce the faint
Half-flush that dies along her throat;' such stuff
Was courtesy, she thought, and cause enough
For calling up that spot of joy. She had
A heart . . . how shall I say ? . . . too soon made glad,
Too easily impressed; she liked whate'er
She looked on, and her looks went everywhere.
Sir, 't was all one! My favour at her breast,
The dropping of the daylight in the West,
The bough of cherries some officious fool
Broke in the orchard for her, the white mule
She rode with round the terrace—all and each
Would draw from her alike the approving speech,
Or blush, at least. She thanked men,—good; but thanked
Somehow . . . I know not how . . . as if she ranked

My gift of a nine-hundred-years-old name
With anybody's gift. Who'd stoop to blame
This sort of trifling? Even had you skill
In speech—(which I have not)—to make your will
Quite clear to such an one, and say 'Just this
Or that in you disgusts me; here you miss,
Or there exceed the mark'—and if she let
Herself be lessoned so, nor plainly set
Her wits to yours, forsooth, and made excuse,
—E'en then would be some stooping, and I chuse
Never to stoop. Oh, Sir, she smiled, no doubt,
Whene'er I passed her; but who passed without
Much the same smile? This grew; I gave commands;
Then all smiles stopped together. There she stands
As if alive. Will't please you rise? we'll meet
The company below, then. I repeat,
The Count your Master's known munificence
Is ample warrant that no just pretence
Of minè for dowry will be disallowed;
Though his fair daughter's self, as I avowed
At starting, is my object. Nay, we'll go
Together down, Sir! Notice Neptune, though,
Taming a sea-horse, thought a rarity,
Which Claus of Innsbruck cast in bronze for me.

ROBERT BROWNING

After this, Jesus left those parts and withdrew into the neighbourhood of Tyre and Sidon. And here a woman, a Chanaanite by birth, who came from that country, cried aloud, "Have pity on me, Lord. My daughter is cruelly troubled by an evil spirit." He gave no word in answer; but His disciples came to him and pleaded with Him: "Rid us of her," they said. "She is following us with her cries." And He answered, "My errand is only to the lost sheep that are the house of Israel." Then the woman came up and said, falling at His feet, "Lord, help me." He answered, "It is not right to take the children's bread and throw it to the dogs." "Ah, yes, Lord," she said, "The dogs feed on the crumbs that fall from their master's table." And at that Jesus answered her, "Woman, for this great faith of thine, let thy will be granted." And from that hour her daughter was cured. (Matthew, 15).

▶ The Phoenician Woman

'She has followed us all day, master, hooknosed, insistent,
Yapping at our heels in commercial Greek:
Her husband a boat-builder—those boats of gopherwood,
Her daughter, it seems, possessed of a devil
Which you, master, a Jew, are supposed to exorcize.
Talk to her, master, send her away.
Tell her you came to the children of Israel,
Not to Phoenician dogs.'

He turned on me sternly. But His voice smiled.
'You hear what they say?' He demanded.
'Is it right, do you think, taking the children's food
And tossing it to the dogs?'

'Master,' I replied, feeling the bond between us,
A humour we shared alone,
'Even dogs are allowed scraps from the table
When the children reject them.'
His face smiled too.
'You have understanding and faith, mother:
'It will happen as you desire'.

It was true. Coming to the hill above Tyre,
Weary beyond all weariness, I fell on my knees,
Letting my eyes search where feet could not follow.
Looking down on the cluster of evening ships,
The causeway with its moving chain of carriers
And the heap of murex-shells outside the dye-works,
I saw her coming from the bazaars to meet me,
Her white conspicuous among blues and purples.
She did not need to speak.
She walked up the hill as a girl walks
Whose arms are her own.

CLIVE SANSOM

gopherwood: cypress
murex: shellfish which yields purple dye.

▶ Night of the Scorpion

I remember the night my mother
was stung by a scorpion. Ten hours
of steady rain had driven him
to crawl beneath a sack of rice.
Parting with his poison—flash
of diabolic tail in the dark room—
he risked the rain again.
The peasants came like swarms of flies
and buzzed the name of God a hundred times
to paralyse the Evil One.
With candles and with lanterns
throwing giant scorpion shadows
on the mud-baked walls
they searched for him: he was not found.
They clicked their tongues.
With every movement that the scorpion made
his poison moved in Mother's blood, they said.
May he sit still, they said.
May the sins of your previous birth
be burned away tonight, they said.
May your suffering decrease
the misfortunes of your next birth, they said.
May the sum of evil
balanced in this unreal world
against the sum of good
become diminished by your pain.
May the poison purify your flesh
of desire, and your spirit of ambition,
they said, and they sat around
on the floor with my mother in the centre,
the peace of understanding on each face.
More candles, more lanterns, more neighbours,
more insects, and the endless rain.

My mother, twisted through and through,
groaning on a mat.
My father, sceptic, rationalist,
trying every curse and blessing,
powder, mixture, herb and hybrid.
He even poured a little paraffin
upon the bitten toe and put a match to it.
I watched the flame feeding on my mother.
I watched the holy man perform his rites
to tame the poison with an incantation.
After twenty hours
it lost its sting.

My mother only said
Thank God the scorpion picked on me
and spared my children.

NISSIM EZEKIEL

▶ Down by the Salley Gardens

Down by the salley gardens my love and I did meet.
She passed the salley gardens with little snow-white feet.
She bid me take love easy, as the leaves grow on the tree;
But I, being young and foolish, with her would not agree.
In a field by the river my love and I did stand,
And on my leaning shoulder she laid her snow-white hand.
She bid me take life easy, as the grass grows on the weirs;
But I was young and foolish, and now am full of tears.

W. B. YEATS

▶ Ballad

Oh, come my joy, my soldier boy,
With your golden buttons, your scarlet coat,
Oh let me play with your twinkling sword
And sail away in your wonderful boat!

The soldier came and took the boy.
Together they marched the dusty roads.
Instead of war, they sang at Fairs,
And mended old chairs with river reeds.

The boy put on a little black patch
And learned to sing on a tearful note;
The soldier sold his twinkling sword
To buy a crutch and jet-black flute.

And when the summer sun rode high
They laughed the length of the shining day;
But when the robin stood in the hedge
The little lad's courage drained away.

Oh soldier, my soldier, take me home
To the nut-brown cottage under the hill.
My mother is waiting, I'm certain sure;
She's far too old to draw at the well!

As snowflakes fell the boy spoke so,
For twenty years, ah twenty years;
But a look in the soldier's eyes said no,
And the roads of England were wet with tears.

One morning, waking on the moors,
The lad laughed aloud at the corpse at his side.
He buried the soldier under a stone,
But kept the flute to soothe his pride.

The days dragged on and he came to a town,
Where he got a red jacket for chopping wood;
And meeting a madman by the way,
He bartered the flute for a twinkling sword.

And so he walked the width of the land
With a warlike air and a jaunty word,
Looking out for a likely lad
With the head of a fool and the heart of a bard.

HENRY TREECE

▶ The Cleveland Lyke Wake Dirge

This ae night, this ae night,
Every night and all;
Fire and selte and candle-light;
And Christ receive thy saule.

When thou from hence away are passed,
Every night and all,
To Whinny-muir thou comest at last;
And Christ receive thy saule.

If ever thou gavest hosen and shoon,
Every night and all,
Sit thee down and put them on;
And Christ receive thy saule.

If hosen and shoon thou ne'er gavest nane,
Every night and all,
The whins shall pyke thee to the bare bane;
And Christ receive thy saule.

From Whinny-muir when thou may'st pass,
Every night and alle,
To Brig o' Dread thou com'st at last;
And Christ receive thy saule.

If ever thou gave of thy silver and gold,
Every night and all,
At Brig o' Dread thou'lt find foothold;
And Christ receive thy saule.

If silver or gold thou ne'er gavest nane,
Every night and all,
Thou'lt tumble down towards hell's flame;
And Christ receive thy saule.

From Brig o' Dread when thou mayest pass,
Every night and all,
To Purgatory fire thou comest at last;
And Christ receive thy saule.

If ever thou gavest meat or drink,
Every night and all,
The fire shall never make thee shrink;
And Christ receive thy saule.

If meat or drink thou ne'er gavest nane,
Every night and all,
The fire shall burn thee to the bare bane;
And Christ receive thy saule.

This ae night, this ae night,
Every night and all,
Fire and selte and candle-light,
And Christ receive thy saule.

ANON.

lyke wake: corpse-watch
ae: one
selte: salt
pyke: pierce

This dirge was sung over corpses, and is particularly associated with the Cleveland district in Yorkshire. Whinny-Muir ('Gorse-Moor') lies near by. A dish of salt was placed on the corpse's breast to keep away the Devil.

▶ Gunpowder Plot

For days these curious cardboard buds have lain
In brightly coloured boxes. Soon the night
Will come. We pray there'll be no sullen rain
To make these magic orchids flame less bright.

Now in the garden's darkness they begin
To flower: the frenzied whizz of Catherine-wheel
Puts forth its fiery petals and the thin
Rocket soars to burst upon the steel

Bulwark of a cloud. And then the guy,
Absurdly human phoenix, is again
Gulped by greedy flames: the harvest sky
Is flecked with threshed and glittering golden grain.

'Uncle! A cannon! Watch me as I light it!'
The women helter-skelter, squealing high,
Retreat; the paper fuse is quickly lit,
A cat-like hiss and spit of fire, a sly

Falter, then the air is shocked with blast.
The cannon bangs and in my nostrils drifts
A bitter scent that brings the lurking past
Lurching to my side. The present shifts,

Allows a ten-year memory to walk
Unhindered now; and so I'm forced to hear
The banshee howl of mortar and the talk
Of men who died; am forced to taste my fear.

I listen for a moment to the guns,
The torn earth's grunts, recalling how I prayed.
The past retreats. I hear a corpse's sons—
'Who's scared of bangers!' 'Uncle, John's afraid!'

VERNON SCANNELL

▶ The Fishers

Two men stood thigh-deep in the sea,
Their bodies braced against the pounding surf,
Hauling a net of fishes;
Heel-deep in shifting sand, inch by inch the fishers neared
the shore,
For heavy was the brown net with sea and fishes,
And the pushing of a great sea-wind against them,
But already gleamed the silver sequins of creatures of the
sea,
Their round eyes goggling, and mouths agape for breath.

The two men leant against the wall of wind,
Calm in the sureness of their plunder,
And one, the taller by a head, cried: 'John,
The net is heavy with big fishes,'
And laughed and hummed a chanty.

But the man John did not hear, for the wind had him,
Whispering the lisp of his dead love of the spring,
The wind whipped him, but the fires of his heart were
drowned,
And the fisher John fished not for fishes,
Nor braced his thighs against the piling sea,
But loosed his tug and let the net go slack,
And the other cried, 'John, the net is loose,'
And urged him stiffen 'gainst the fish escape.

The man John heard the voice as one hears shells
Murmuring of things long gone—
Irredeemable springs, and love's laughter dead,
And John the fisher let his net-hold go,
And a great surf took his feet, and tangled them,
Wrapping him to his thighs in twisted flax,
And drew him down,

And sucked him to the deeps.
The net unbent its brown salt length,
And heavy of its trove of man and fishes,
Came shorewards inch by inch to ankle shallows.

While John the fisher lay so still upon the sands,
The fishes quivered, then blindly stared;
So stared the man John—at some far nothingness,
Where the fishes' breath slept, and his one spring song.

BRIAN VREPONT

▶ Dulce et Decorum Est

Bent double, like old beggars under sacks,
Knock-kneed, coughing like hags, we cursed though sludge,
Till on the haunting flares we turned our backs,
And towards our distant rest began to trudge.
Men marched asleep. Many had lost their boots,
But limped on, blood-shod. All went lame, all blind;
Drunk with fatigue; deaf even to the hoots
Of gas-shells dropping softly behind.

Gas! GAS! Quick, boys!—An ecstasy of fumbling,
Fitting the clumsy helmets just in time,
But someone still was yelling out and stumbling
And floundering like a man in fire or lime.—
Dim through the misty panes and thick green light,
As under a green sea, I saw him drowning.
In all my dreams before my helpless sight
He plunges at me, guttering, choking, drowning.

If in some smothering dreams, you too could pace
Behind the wagon that we flung him in,
And watch the white eyes writhing in his face,
His hanging face, like a devil's sick of sin;
If you could hear, at every jolt, the blood
Come gargling from the froth-corrupted lungs,
Bitter as the cud
Of vile, incurable sores on innocent tongues,—
My friend, you would not tell with such high zest
To children ardent for some desperate glory,
The old Lie: Dulce et decorum est
Pro patria mori.†

WILFRED OWEN

† To die for one's country is a fine and fitting thing (Horace *Odes*)

▶ Tam o' Shanter

When chapman billies leave the street,
And drouthy neebors neebors meet;
As market-days are wearing late,
An' folk begin to tak the gate;
While we sit bousing at the nappy
An' getting fou and unco happy,
We think na on the lang Scots miles,
The mosses, waters, slaps, and stiles,
That lie between us and our hame,
Whare sits our sulky sullen dame,
Gathering her brows like gathering storm,
Nursing her wrath to keep it warm.

This truth fand honest Tam o' Shanter,
As he frae Ayr ae night did canter:
(Auld Ayr, wham ne'er a town surpasses
For honest men and bonnie lasses).

O Tam! hadst thou but been sae wise
As taen thy ain wife Kate's advice!
She tauld thee weel thou was a skellum,
A blethering, blustering, drunken blellum;
That frae November till October,
Ae market-day thou was nae sober;
That ilka melder wi' the miller
Thou sat as lang as thou had siller;

chapman billies: pedlars *drouthy:* thirsty
gate: road *bousing at the nappy:* drinking ale
unco: very *slaps:* gates *fand:* found
skellum: rogue *blellum:* idle babbler
ilka melder: every meal-grinding *siller:* silver

That every naig was ca'd a shoe on
The smith and thee gat roaring fou on;
That at the Lord's house, even on Sunday,
Thou drank wi' Kirkton Jean till Monday.
She prophesied that, late or soon,
Thou would be found deep drown'd in Doon;
Or catched wi' warlocks in the mirk
By Alloway's auld haunted kirk.

Ah, gentle dames! it gars me greet
To think how monie counsels sweet,
How monie lengthen'd, sage advices
The husband frae the wife despises!

But to our tale:—Ae market-night,
Tam had got planted unco right;
Fast by an ingle, bleezing finely,
Wi' reaming swats, that drank divinely;

And at his elbow, Souter Johnie,
His ancient, trusty, drouthy cronie;
Tam lo'ed him like a very brither;
They had been fou for weeks thegither.
The night drave on wi' sangs and clatter;
And ay the ale was growing better:
The landlady and Tam grew gracious
Wi' favours secret, sweet, and precious:
The Souter tauld his queerest stories
The landlord's laugh was ready chorus:
The storm without might rair and rustle,
Tam did na mind the storm a whistle.

fou: drunk *gars me greet:* makes me weep
ingle: fire *reaming swats:* foaming new ale
Souter: cobbler *rair:* roar

Care, mad to see a man sae happy,
E'en drown'd himsel amang the nappy:
As bees flee hame wi' lades o' treasure,
The minutes wing'd their way wi' pleasure:
Kings may be blest, but Tam was glorious,
O'er a' the ills o' life victorious!
But pleasures are like poppies spread,
You seize the flow'r, its bloom is shed;
Or like the snow falls in the river,
A moment white—then melts for ever;
Or like the borealis race,
That flit ere you can point their place;
Or like the rainbow's lovely form
Evanishing amid the storm.—
Nae man can tether time or tide;
The hour approaches Tam maun ride;
That hour, o' night's black arch the key-stane
That dreary hour he mounts his beast in;
And sic a night he taks the road in,
As ne'er poor sinner was abroad in.

The wind blew as 'twad blawn its last;
The rattling showers rose on the blast;
The speedy gleams the darkness swallow'd;
Loud, deep, and lang, the thunder bellow'd:
That night, a child might understand,
The Deil had business on his hand.

Weel mounted on his grey mare, Meg,
A better never lifted leg,
Tam skelpit on thro' dub and mire,
Despising wind, and rain, and fire;

nappy: ale   *skelpit:* battled   *dub:* puddle

Whiles holding fast his gude blue bonnet;
Whiles crooning o'er some auld Scots sonnet;
Whiles glowring round wi' prudent cares,
Lest bogles catch him unawares:
Kirk-Alloway was drawing nigh,
Whare ghaists and houlets nightly cry.—

By this time he was cross the ford,
Whare in the snaw the chapman smoor'd;
And past the birks and meikle stane,
Whare drunken Charlie brak's neck-bane;
And thro' the whins, and by the cairn
Whare hunters fand the murder'd bairn;
And near the thorn, aboon the well,
Whare Mungo's mither hang'd hersel.
Before him Doon pours all his floods,
The doubling storm roars thro' the woods;
The lightnings flash from pole to pole;
Near and more near the thunders roll:
When, glimmering thro' the groaning trees,
Kirk-Alloway seem'd in a bleeze;
Thro' ilka bore the beams were glancing;
And loud resounded mirth and dancing.

Inspiring bold John Barleycorn!
What dangers thou canst make us scorn!
Wi' tippenny we fear nae evil;
Wi' usquabae we'll face the Devil!

bogles: ghosts   *houlets:* owlets
smoor'd: smothered   *birks:* birches   *meikle:* big
whins: gorse   *ilka bore:* every cranny
tippenny: light ale   *usquabae:* whisky

The swats sae ream'd in Tammie's noddle.
Fair play, he car'd na deils a boddle.
But Maggie stood right sair astonish'd,
Till, by the heel and hand admonish'd,
She ventur'd forward on the light;
And, wow! Tam saw an unco sight!

Warlocks and witches in a dance;
Nae cotillion brent-new frae France,
But hornpipes, jigs, strathspeys and reels,
Put life and mettle in their heels,
A winnock-bunker in the east,
There sat Auld Nick, in shape o' beast;
A towsie tyke, black, grim and large,
To gie them music was his charge:
He screw'd the pipes and gart them skirl
Till roof and rafters a' did dirl.
Coffins stood round, like open presses,
That shaw'd the dead in their last dresses;
And, by some devilish cantraip sleight,
Each in its cauld hand held a light—
By which heroic Tam was able
To note upon the haly table
A murderer's banes in gibbet airns;
Twa span-lang, wee, unchristen'd bairns;
A thief, new-cutted frae a rape,
Wi' his last gasp his gab did gape;
Five tomahawks, wi' blude red-rusted;
Five scymitars, wi' murder crusted;

swats: ale   *ream'd:* frothed   *boddle:* farthing
unco: marvellous   *warlock:* goblin
brent-new: brand new   *winnock-bunker:* window recess
towsie tyke: shaggy dog   *gart:* made
dirl: vibrate   *cantraip:* magic   *haly:* holy
airns: irons   *rape:* rope

A garter, which a babe had strangled;
A knife, a father's throat had mangled,
Whom his ain son o' life bereft,
The grey hairs yet stack to the heft;
Wi' mair o' horrible and awefu',
Which even to name wad be unlawfu'.

As Tammie glowr'd, amaz'd, and curious,
The mirth and fun grew fast and furious:
The piper loud and louder blew;
The dancers quick and quicker flew;
They reel'd, they set, they cross'd, they cleekit,
Till ilka carlin swat and reekit,
And coost her duddies to the wark,
And linket at it in her sark!

Now, Tam, O Tam! had thae been queans,
A' plump and strapping in their teens,
Their sarks, instead o' creeshie flannen,
Been snaw-white seventeen hundred linnen!
Thir breeks o' mine, my only pair,
That ance were plush, o' gude blue hair,
I wad hae gi'en them off my hurdies,
For ae blink o' the bonnie burdies!

But wither'd beldams, auld and droll,
Rigwoodie hags wad spean a foal,
Lowping and flinging on a crummock,
I wonder didna turn thy stomach.

cleekit: linked arms   *carlin:* witch
swat: sweated   *coost:* cast off   *duddies:* clothes
wark: work   *sark:* shift   *queans:* young women
creeshie flannen: greasy flannel
hurdies: buttocks   *burdies:* girls
rigwoodie: wizened   *spean:* wean
crummock: stick

But Tam kend what was what fu' brawlie,
There was ae winsome wench and wawlie,
That night enlisted in the core,
(Lang after kend on Carrick shore;
For mony a beast to dead she shot,
And perish'd mony a bonnie boat,
And shook baith meikle corn and bear,
And held the country-side in fear).
Her cutty sark, o' Paisley harn,
That while a lassie she had worn,
In longitude tho' sorely scanty,
It was her best, and she was vauntie.—
Ah! little kend thy reverend grannie,
That sark she coft for her wee Nannie,
Wi' twa pund Scots ('twas a' her riches),
Wad ever grac'd a dance of witches!
But here my Muse her wing maun cour
Sic flights are far beyond her pow'r;
To sing how Nannie lap and flang
(A souple jade she was and strang),
And how Tam stood like ane bewitch'd
And thought his very een enrich'd;
Even Satan glowr'd, and fidg'd fu' fain,
And hotch'd and blew wi' might and main,
Till first ae caper, syne anither,
Tam tint his reason a' thegither
And roars out: 'Weel done, Cutty-sark!'
And in an instant all was dark;
And scarcely had he Maggie rallied,
When out the hellish legion sallied.

brawlie: well   *ae:* one   *wawlie:* comely
bear: barley   *cutty sark:* short shift
Paisley harn: coarse linen   *vauntie:* proud of it
coft: bought   *cour:* fold   *lap:* leaped
flang: kicked   *fidg'd:* fidgeted
hotch'd: squirmed   *syne:* then   *tint:* lost

183

As bees bizz out wi' angry fyke,
When plundering herds assail their byke;
As open pussie's mortal foes,
When, pop! she starts before their nose;
As eager runs the market-crowd,
When 'Catch the thief!' resounds aloud;
So Maggie runs, the witches follow,
Wi' monie an eldritch skriech and hollow.

Ah, Tam! Ah, Tam! thou'll get thy fairin'!
In hell they'll roast thee like a herrin'!
In vain thy Kate awaits thy comin'!
Kate soon will be a woefu' woman!
Now, do thy speedy utmost, Meg,
And win the key-stane of the brig,
There, at them thou thy tail may toss:
A running stream they dare na cross.

But ere the key-stane she could make,
The fient a tail she had to shake!
For Nannie, far before the rest,
Hard upon noble Maggie prest,
And flew at Tam wi' furious ettle;
But little wist she Maggie's mettle—
Ae spring brought off her master hale,
But left behind her ain grey tail:
The carlin claught her by the rump,
And left poor Maggie scarce a stump.

Now, wha this tale o' truth shall read,
Ilk man and mother's son, take heed:

fyke: fret   *herds:* herd-boys   *byke:* hive
pussie: hare   *eldritch:* unearthly
fairin': reward   *brig:* bridge
ettle: endeavour

184

Whene'er to drink you are inclin'd,
Or cutty-sarks run in your mind,
Think, ye may buy the joys o'er dear,
Remember Tam o' Shanter's mare.

ROBERT BURNS

▶ To an Isle in the Water

Shy one, shy one,
Shy one of my heart,
She moves in the firelight
Pensively apart.

She carries in the dishes,
And lays them in a row.
To an isle in the water
With her would I go.

She carries in the candles,
And lights the curtained room,
Shy in the doorway
And shy in the gloom;

And shy as a rabbit,
Helpful and shy.
To an isle in the water
With her would I fly.

W. B. YEATS

▶ One Who Married Above Him

''Tis you, I think? Back from your week's work, Steve?'
'It is I. Back from work this Christmas Eve.'
'But you seem off again?—in this night-rime?'
'I am off again, and thoroughly off this time.'
    'What does that mean?'
    'More than may first be seen . . . .
Half an hour ago I footed homeward here,
No wife found I, nor child, nor maid, indoors or near.
She has, as always, gone with them to her mother's at the
    farm,
Where they fare better far than here, and, maybe, meet less
    harm.
She's left no fire, no light, has cooked me nothing to eat,
Though she had fuel, and money to get some Christmas
    meat.
Christmas with them is grand, she knows, and brings good
    victual,
Other than how it is here, where it's but lean and little.
    But though not much, and rough,
    If managed neat there's enough.
    She and hers are too highmade for me;
    But she's whimmed her once too often, she'll see!
Farmer Bollen's daughter should never have married a man
    that's poor;
And I can stand it no longer; I'm leaving; you'll see me no
    more, be sure.'
'But nonsense! You'll be back again ere bedtime, and light-
    ing a fire,
And sizzling your supper, and vexing not that her views of
    supper are higher.'
    'Never for me.'
    'Well, we shall see.'
The sceptical neighbour and Stephen then followed their
    fore-designed ways,

And their steps dimmed into white silence upon the slippery
  glaze;
And the trees went on with their spitting amid the icicled
  haze.

The evening whiled, and the wife with the babies came
  home,
But he was not there, nor all Christmas Day did he come.
Christmastide went, and likewise went the New Year,
But no husband's footfall revived,
And month after month lapsed, graytime to green and to
  sere,
And other new years arrived,
And the children grew up: one husbanded and one wived.—

    She wept and repented,
  But Stephen never relented.
And there stands the house, and the sycamore-tree and all
With its roots forming steps for the passers who care to call,
And there are the mullioned windows, and Ham-Hill door,
Through which Steve's wife was brought out, but which
  Steve re-entered no more.

THOMAS HARDY

▶ To Althea, from Prison

When Love with unconfinèd wings
   Hovers within my gates;
And my divine Althea brings
   To whisper at the grates:
When I lie tangled in her hair,
   And fettered to her eye;
The birds, that wanton in the air,
   Know no such liberty.

When flowing cups run swiftly round
   With no allaying Thames,
Our careless heads with roses bound,
   Our hearts with loyal flames;
When thirsty grief in wine we steep,
   When healths and draughts go free,
Fishes that tipple in the deep,
   Know no such liberty.

When (like committed linnets) I
   With shriller throat shall sing
The sweetness, mercy, majesty,
   And glories of my King;
When I shall voice aloud, how good
   He is, how great should be;
Enlargèd winds that curl the flood,
   Know no such liberty.

Stone walls do not a prison make,
   Nor iron bars a cage,
Minds innocent and quiet take
   That for an hermitage;
If I have freedom in my love,
   And in my soul am free;
Angels alone that soar above,
   Enjoy such liberty.

RICHARD LOVELACE

▶ Anecdote

Perhaps she cared too much
For her own company. Perhaps
Even her own company
Was too much for her. Anyway,
She lived to herself in a house in a walled garden
So neglected now
That the house was scarcely visible
Through the wild trees that lolled over the wall.

She had little to do with the villagers
Though all agreed
That whenever they chanced to have a word with her
She was friendly enough in a way:
It was simply that no word
However pleasantly spoken
Was able to cross the barrier between them—
There was always the wall.

And yet
It seemed that even a wall
Could not keep out whatever it was she feared.

One evening in May
When the wild trees bloomed like clouds
Blowing over the garden
And Spring gave promise of more
Than ever Spring could possibly perform,
Two men met under the wall
And stayed to pass the time of day,
Made fellow by the benign mood of the hour.
And as they talked
A blackbird opened his throat in the blossoming trees
And sang so sweet and mellow
The music gathered all to itself;
And they could do no other than pause and listen.

Suddenly
A window was flung open in the house
And almost before the men knew what was happening
The crack of a gun had snapped the song asunder
Like a broken stick,
And a voice from the stunned silence after
Asked, 'Did I get it?'
But would not wait for an answer.
The window closed again. The two men smiled
And went their ways, bidding each other Good-night.

C. HENRY WARREN

▶ Hillside Burial

Between the dry stone walling of a hill
twelve men are burying a neighbour,
their bare heads barren as boulders,
their throats brittle as dead heather.

There is no priest, ceremony, flowers,
only the shepherds' granite words
committing one of their own kind
to the dark field beyond earth's boundary.

And as they lock his body from the sun
with soil and pebbles of his native land,
each feels the emptiness and loss
left in their fingers by the falling stone.

EDWARD STOREY

▶ Culloden: The Last Battle

The black cloud crumbled.

My plaid that Morag wove
In Drumnakiel, three months before the eagle
Fell in the West, clung like the grey sea hag
Around my blood.

We sat on the starved moor
And broke our last round bannock.

Fergus Mor
Was praying to every crossed and beaded saint
That swung Iona like the keel of Scotland
Into the wrecking European wave.
Gow shook his flask. Alastair sang out
He would be drunker still on German blood
Before the hawk was up: for 'Look' cried he
'At all the hogsheads waiting to be tapped
Among the rocks!'

Old ironmouth spilled his brimstone,
Nodded, and roared. Then all were at their texts,
And Fergus fell, and Donald gave a cry
Like a wounded stag, and raised his steel and leaped
Into the pack. But we were hunters too,
All smoking tongues. I picked my chosen quarry
Between the squares. Morag at her wheel,
Turning the fog of wool to a thin swift line
Of August light, drew me to love no surer
Than that red man to war. And his cold stance
Seemed to expect my coming. We had hastened
Faithful as brothers from the sixth cry of God
To play this game of ghost on the long moor.
His eye was hard as dice, his cheek was cropped

For the far tryst, his English bayonet
Bright as a wolf's tooth. Our wild paths raced together,
Locked in the heather, faltered by the white stone,
Then mine went on alone.

      'Come back, come back,'
Alastair cried.
      I turned.
      Three red shapes
Drifted about me in the drifting smoke.
We crossed like dreams.
      This was the last battle.
We had not turned before.
      The eagle was up
And away to the isles.
      That night we lay
Far in the west. Alastair died on the straw.
We travelled homeward, on the old lost roads,
Twilight by twilight, shepherd by weeping shepherd.

My three wounds were heavy and round as medals
Till Morag broke them with her long fingers.

Weaving, she sings of the beauty of defeat.

GEORGE MACKAY BROWN

The battle here is Culloden, 1746, where the Highland troops
under Charles Edward Stewart Bonnie Prince Charlie, were
crushed by an English army led by the Duke of Cumberland.
Without cannon, and outnumbered two to one, the Highlanders
were routed and the Jacobite cause lost.
Then all were at their texts: The soldier speaking is a Calvinist and
the English cannon reminds him of a minister thundering out of
the pulpit.
from the sixth cry of God: God made men on the sixth day of the
Creation. The Scottish soldier and his English adversary were
predestined to meet on this battlefield.

▶ The New Admission

The telephone bell rang out, untimely, shrill:
A sound to freeze the will,
Like a bugle call over tents of the dead—
We patients huddled, and lay still.
We knew full well what the summons heralded;
But pity in our hearts had died
Along with ardour and resolve;
We did not move
While the nurse prepared another bed.
'A new admission,' someone lightly said.

And presently, through the fateful door,
She came, a nurse at either side,
Her wild gaze fixed, and her long hair
Wreathed in wet bands about her head,
Her nightgown trailing out behind;
Like some ship's effigy of womankind
Washed from a subterranean floor
To gaze unwittingly once more
Over an alien shore . . .
'Could anyone,' asked the nurse, 'spare
A comb?'
And wiped from those pale, wooden lips
A trace of foam.

She lay as they put her, murmuring of home,
Over and over, hour by hour.
We felt for her as one would feel
For a caged mouse running in a wire wheel;
But there was nothing to be done.
'Admission Ward, Female, One'
Would be her address for a long time to come.

O. M. SALTER

▶ The Black Ape

The black ape's principal food is fruit,
They are fond of attention and quite docile,
When they are pleased they expose their teeth
In a way very like a human smile,

They are known to have bred in captivity,
In the Javan forests they are found in groups.
Pongo was given a cage to himself
Fitted with swings and ropes with loops.

Every day the children would watch him swing
Or climb the spokes of his turning wheel.
They always peeled his bananas and pears
Although he seemed to like the peel.

One Tuesday in August Pongo broke out,
Climbed over the roofs and played scapegrace.
He stole some fruit but was still hungry,
And teased by a child he scratched its face.

A crowd gathered with umbrellas and rakes
And cornered him in a small bathroom,
Pongo grew savage. The police took charge
And decided to administer chloroform.

They discovered the owner's name at last,
And a taxidermist stuffed the skin.
A zoologist questioned on TV
Affirmed that in zoos they are well locked in.

The black ape's principal food is fruit,
They are fond of attention and quite docile,
When they are pleased they expose their teeth
In a way very like a human smile.

LEO AYLEN

▶ The Gallows

There was a weasel lived in the sun
With all his family,
Till a keeper shot him with his gun
And hung him up on a tree,
Where he swings in the wind and rain,
In the sun and in the snow,
Without pleasure, without pain,
On the dead oak tree bough.

There was a crow who was no sleeper,
But a thief and a murderer
Till a very late hour; and this keeper
Made him one of the things that were,
To hang and flap in rain and wind,
In the sun and in the snow.
There are no more sins to be sinned
On the dead oak tree bough.

There was a magpie, too,
Had a long tongue and a long tail;
He could both talk and do—
But what did that avail?
He, too, flaps in the wind and rain
Alongside weasel and crow,
Without pleasure, without pain,
On the dead oak tree bough.

And many other beasts
And birds, skin, bone and feather,
Have been taken from their feasts
And hung up there together,
To swing and have endless leisure
In the sun and in the snow,
Without pain, without pleasure,
On the dead oak tree bough.

EDWARD THOMAS

▶ Time of Roses

It was not in the Winter
   Our loving lot was cast;
It was the time of roses—
We pluck'd them as we pass'd!

That churlish season never frown'd
   On early lovers yet:
O no—the world was newly crown'd
   With flowers when first we met!

'Twas twilight, and I bade you go,
   But still you held me fast;
It was the time of roses—
   We pluck'd them as we pass'd.

THOMAS HOOD

▶ The fox-coloured pheasant enjoyed his peace

The fox-coloured pheasant enjoyed his peace,
there were no labourers in the wheat,
dogs were stretched out at ease,
the empty road echoed my feet.

It was the time for owls' voices,
trees were dripping dark like rain,
and sheep made night-time noises
as I went down the hill lane.

In the streets of the still town
I met a man in the lamplight,
he stood in the alley that led down
to the harbour and the sea out of sight.

Who do you want? he asked me,
Who are you looking for in this place?
The houses echoed us emptily
and the lamp shone on his face.

Does your girl live here?
(There were no girls or sailors about.)
I have no girl anywhere,
I want a ship putting out.

He stood under the lamplight
and I stepped up close to him,
his eyes burned like fires at night
and the lamp seemed dim.

He came closer up and pressed
his crooked knee to my knee,
and his chest to my chest,
and held my shoulders and wrestled with me.

It was the middle time of night
with five hours to run till day,
but the sky was crimson and bright
before he stood out of my way.

I ran past as quick as I could
and the wet stones rang loudly
along the wharf where the ships stood
and the sea lifting proudly.

PETER LEVI

The poem may be interpreted on several levels: an attack on a
sailor on his way back to his ship; man struggles with death; a
doubting soul fights for faith in God. The poet himself has
referred to the Bible story of Jacob wrestling with the angel.

▶ Rondeau

Jenny kissed me when we met,
   Jumping from the chair she sat in;
Time you thief, who love to get
   Sweets into your list, put that in!
Say I'm weary, say I'm sad,
   Say that health and wealth have missed me,
Say I'm growing old, but add,
   Jenny kiss'd me.

LEIGH HUNT

▶ Pike

Pike, three inches long, perfect
Pike in all parts, green tigering the gold.
Killers from the egg: the malevolent aged grin.
They dance on the surface among the flies.

Or move, stunned by their own grandeur,
Over a bed of emerald, silhouette
Of submarine delicacy and horror.
A hundred feet long in their world.

In ponds, under the heat-struck lily pads—
Gloom of their stillness:
Logged on last year's black leaves, watching upwards.
Or hung in an amber cavern of weeds

The jaws' hooked clamp and fangs
Not to be changed at this date;
A life subdued to its instrument;
The gills kneading quietly, and the pectorals.

Three we kept behind glass,
Jungled in weed: three inches, four,
And four and a half: fed fry to them—
Suddenly there were two. Finally one

With a sag belly and the grin it was born with.
And indeed they spare nobody.
Two, six pounds each, over two feet long,
High and dry and dead in the willow-herb—

One jammed past its gills down the other's gullet:
The outside eye stared: as a vice locks—
The same iron in this eye
Though its film shrank in death.

A pond I fished, fifty yards across,
Whose lilies and muscular tench
Had outlasted every visible stone
Of the monastery that planted them—

Stilled legendary depth:
It was as deep as England. It held
Pike too immense to stir, so immense and old
That past nightfall I dared not cast

But silently cast and fished
With the hair frozen on my head
For what might move, for what eye might move.
The still splashes on the dark pond,

Owls hushing the floating woods
Frail on my ear against the dream
Darkness beneath night's darkness had freed,
That rose slowly towards me, watching.

TED HUGHES

► London

I wander thro' each charter'd street,
Near where the charter'd Thames does flow,
And mark in every face I meet
Marks of weakness, marks of woe.

In every cry of every Man,
In every Infant's cry of fear,
In every voice, in every ban,
The mind-forg'd manacles I hear.

How the Chimney-sweeper's cry
Every black'ning Church appals;
And the hapless Soldier's sigh
Runs in blood down Palace walls.

But most thro' midnight streets I hear
How the youthful Harlot's curse
Blasts the new born Infant's tear,
And blights with plagues the Marriage hearse.

WILLIAM BLAKE

▶ The Thing

Suddenly they came flying, like a long scarf of smoke,
Trailing a thing—what was it?—small as a lark
Above the blue air, in the slight haze beyond.
A thing in and out of sight,
Flashing between gold levels of the late sun,
Then throwing itself up and away from the implacable
  swift pursuers.

Confusing them once flying straight into the sun
So they circled aimlessly for almost a minute,
Only to find, with their long terrible eyes
The small thing diving down toward a hill,
Where they dropped again
In one streak of pursuit.

Then the first bird
Struck;
Then another, another,
Until there was nothing left,
Not even feathers from so far away.

And we turned to our picnic
Of veal soaked in marsala and little larks arranged on
  a long platter
And we drank the dry harsh wine
While I poked with a stick at a stone near a four-pronged
  flower,
And a black bull nudged at a wall in the valley below,
And the blue air darkened.

THEODORE ROETHKE

▶ Landscape as Werewolf

Near here, the last grey wolf
In England was clubbed down. Still,
After two hundred years, the same pinched wind
Rakes through his cairn of bones

As he squats quiet, watching daylight seep
Away from the scarred granite, and its going drain
The hills' bare faces. Far below,
A tiny bus twists on its stringy path
And scuttles home around a darkening bend.

The fells contract, regroup in starker forms;
Dusk tightens on them, as the wind gets up
And stretches hungrily: tensed at the nape,
The coarse heath bristles like a living pelt.

The sheep are all penned in. Down at the pub
They sing, and shuttle darts: the hostellers
Dubbin their heavy boots. Above the crags
The first stars prick their eyes and bide their time.

WILLIAM DUNLOP

▶ The Patriot

It was roses, roses, all the way,
   With myrtle mixed in my path like mad:
The house-roofs seemed to heave and sway,
   The church-spires flamed, such flags they had,
A year ago on this very day!

The air broke into a mist with bells,
   The old walls rocked with the crowd and cries.
Had I said, 'Good folk, mere noise repels—
   But give me your sun from yonder skies!'
They had answered, 'And afterward, what else?'

Alack, it was I who leaped at the sun,
   To give it my loving friends to keep!
Nought man could do have I left undone,
   And you see my harvest, what I reap,
This very day, now a year is run.

There's nobody on the house-tops now—
   Just a palsied few at the windows set—
For the best of the sight is, all allow,
   At the Shambles' Gate—or, better yet,
By the very scaffold's foot, I trow.

I go in the rain, and, more than needs,
   A rope cuts both my wrists behind;
And I think, by the feel, my forehead bleeds,
   For they fling, whoever has a mind,
Stones at me for my year's misdeeds.

Thus I entered, and thus I go!
   In triumphs, people have dropped down dead.
'Paid by the world, what dost thou owe
   Me?'—God might question; now instead,
'Tis God shall repay: I am safer so.

ROBERT BROWNING

▶ To Celia

Drink to me only with thine eyes,
And I will pledge with mine;
Or leave a kiss but in the cup
And I'll not look for wine.
The thirst that from the soul doth rise
Doth ask a drink divine;
But might I of Jove's nectar sup,
I would not change for thine.

I sent thee late a rosy wreath,
Not so much honouring thee
As giving it a hope that there
It could not wither'd be;
But thou thereon didst only breathe,
And sent'st it back to me;
Since when it grows, and smells, I swear,
Not of itself, but thee!

BEN JONSON

▶ The Sacrilege

'I have a Love I love too well
Where Dunkery frowns on Exon Moor;
I have a Love I love too well,
   To whom 'ere she was mine,
"Such is my love for you," I said,
"That you shall have to hood your head
A silken kerchief crimson-red,
Wove finest of the fine."

'And since this Love, for one mad moon,
On Exon Wild by Dunkery Tor,
Since this my Love for one mad moon
   Did clasp me as her king,
I snatched a silk-piece red and rare
From off a stall at Priddy Fair.
For handkerchief to hood her hair
   When we went gallanting.

'Full soon the four weeks neared their end
Where Dunkery frowns on Exon Moor;
And when the four weeks neared their end,
   And their swift sweets outwore,
I said, "What shall I do to own
Those beauties bright as tulips blown,
And keep you here with me alone
   And mine for evermore?"

'And as she drowsed within my van
On Exon Wild by Dunkery Tor—
And as she drowsed within my van,
   And dawning turned to day,
She heavily raised her sloe-black eyes
And murmured back in softest wise,
"One more thing, and the charms you prize
   Are yours henceforth for aye.

"And swear I will I'll never go
While Dunkery frowns on Exon Moor
To meet the Cornish Wrestler Joe
   For dance and dallyings.
If you'll to yon cathedral shrine,
And finger from the chest divine
Treasures to buy me ear-drops fine,
   And richly-jewelled rings."

'I said: "I am one who has gathered gear
From Marlbury Downs to Dunkery Tor,
Who has gathered gear for many a year
   From mansion, mart and fair;
But at God's house I've stayed my hand,
Hearing within me some command—
Curbed by a law not of the land
   From doing damage there!"

'Whereat she pouts, this Love of mine,
As Dunkery pouts to Exon Moor,
And still she pouts, this Love of mine,
   So cityward I go.
But ere I start to do the thing,
And speed my soul's imperilling
For one who is my ravishing
   And all the joy I know,

'I come to lay this charge on thee—
On Exon Wild by Dunkery Tor—
I come to lay this charge on thee
   With solemn speech and sign:
Should things go ill, and my life pay
For botchery in this rash assay,
You are to take hers likewise—yea,
The month the law takes mine.

'For should my rival, Wrestler Joe,
Where Dunkery frowns on Exon Moor—
My reckless rival, Wrestler Joe,
    My Love's bedwinner be,
My rafted spirit would not rest,
But wander weary and distrest
Throughout the world in wild protest:
    The thought nigh maddens me!'

'Thus did he speak—this brother of mine——
On Exon Moor by Dunkery Tor,
Born at my birth of mother of mine,
    And forthwith went his way
To dare the deed some coming night . . .
I kept the watch with shaking sight,
The moon at moments breaking bright,
    At others glooming gray.

'For three full days I heard no sound
Where Dunkery frowns on Exon Moor,
I heard no sound at all around
    Whether his fay prevailed,
Or one more foul the master were,
Till some afoot did tidings bear
How that, for all his practised care,
    He had been caught and jailed.

'They had heard a crash when twelve had chimed
    By Mendip east of Dunkery Tor,
When twelve had chimed and moonlight climbed;
    They watched, and he was tracked
By arch and aisle and saint and knight
Of sculptured stonework sheeted white
In the cathedral's ghostly light,
    And captured in the act.

'Yes; for this Love he loved too well
Where Dunkery sights the Severn shore,
All for this Love he loved too well
    He burst the holy bars,
Seized golden vessels from the chest
To buy her ornaments of the best,
At her ill-witchery's request
    And lure of eyes like stars. . . .

'When blustering March confused the sky
In Toneborough Town by Exon Moor,
When blustering March confused the sky
    They stretched him; and he died.
Down in the crowd where I, to see
The end of him, stood silently,
With a set face he lipped to me—
    "Remember." "Ay!" I cried.

'By night and day I shadowed her
From Toneborough Deane to Dunkery Tor,
I shadowed her asleep, astir,
    And yet I could not bear—
Till Wrestler Joe anon began
To figure as her chosen man,
And took her to his shining van—
    To doom a form so fair!

'He made it handsome for her sake—
And Dunkery smiled to Exon Moor—
He made it handsome for her sake,
    Painting it out and in;
And on the door of apple-green
A bright brass knocker soon was seen,
And window-curtains white and clean
    For her to sit within.

'And all could see she clave to him
As cleaves a cloud to Dunkery Tor,
Yea, all could see she clave to him,
    And every day I said,
"A pity it seems to part those two
That hourly grow to love more true:
Yet she's the wanton woman who
    Sent one to swing till dead!"

'That blew to blazing all my hate,
While Dunkery frowned on Exon Moor,
And when the river swelled, her fate
    Came to her pitilessly . . .
I dogged her, crying: "Across that plank
They use as bridge to reach yon bank
A coat and hat lie limp and dank;
    Your goodman's, can they be?"

'She paled, and went, I close behind—
And Exon frowned to Dunkery Tor,
She went, and I came up behind
    And tipped the plank that bore
Her, fleetly flitting across to eye
What such might bode. She slid awry;
And from the current came a cry,
    A gurgle; and no more.

'How that befell no mortal knew
From Marlbury Downs to Exon Moor;
No mortal knew that deed undue
    But he who schemed the crime,
Which night still covers . . . But in dream
Those ropes of hair upon the stream
He sees, and he will hear that scream
    Until his judgment-time.'

THOMAS HARDY

▶ Au Jardin des Plantes

The gorilla lay on his back,
One hand cupped under his head,
Like a man.

Like a labouring man tired with work,
A strong man with his strength burnt away
In the toil of earning a living.

Only of course he was not tired out with work,
Merely with boredom; his terrible strength
All burnt away by prodigal idleness.

A thousand days, and then a thousand days,
Idleness licked away his beautiful strength
He having no need to earn a living.

It was all laid on, free of charge.
We maintained him, not for doing anything,
But for being what he was.

And so that Sunday morning he lay on his back,
Like a man, like a worn-out man,
One hand cupped under his terrible hard head.

Like a man, like a man,
One of those we maintain, not for doing anything,
But for being what they are.

A thousand days, and then a thousand days,
With everything laid on, free of charge,
They cup their heads in prodigal idleness.

JOHN WAIN

Au Jardin des Plantes: At the Paris zoo

▶ May 23

There never was a finer day,
And never will be while May is May,—
The third, and not the last of its kind;
But though fair and clear the two behind
Seemed pursued by tempests overpast;
And the morrow with fear that it could not last
Was spoiled. Today ere the stones were warm
Five minutes of thunderstorm
Dashed it with rain, as if to secure,
By one tear, its beauty the luck to endure.

At midday then along the lane
Old Jack Norman appeared again,
Jaunty and old, crooked and tall,
And stopped and grinned at me over the wall,
With a cowslip bunch in his buttonhole
And one in his cap. Who could say if his roll
Came from flints in the road, the weather, or ale?
He was welcome as the nightingale.

Not an hour of the sun had been wasted on Jack.
'I've got my Indian complexion back,'
Said he. He was tanned like a harvester,
Like his short clay pipe, like the leaf and bur
That clung to his coat from last night's bed,
Like the ploughland crumbling red.
Fairer flowers were none on the earth
Than his cowslips wet with the dew of their birth,
Or fresher leaves than the cress in his basket.
'Where did they come from, Jack?' 'Don't ask it,
And you'll be told no lies.' 'Very well:
Then I can't buy.' 'I don't want to sell,
Take them and these flowers, too, free.

Perhaps you have something to give me?
Wait till next time. The better the day . . . . .
The Lord couldn't make a better, I say;
If He could, He never has done.'
So off went Jack with his roll-walk-run,
Leaving his cresses from Oakshot rill
And his cowslips from Wheatham hill.

'Twas the first day that the midges bit;
But though they bit me, I was glad of it:
Of the dust in my face, too, I was glad.
Spring could do nothing to make me sad.
Bluebells hid all the ruts in the copse,
The elm seeds lay in the road like hops,
That fine day, May the twenty-third,
The day Jack Norman disappeared.

EDWARD THOMAS

▶ Anthem for Doomed Youth

What passing-bells for these who die as cattle?
Only the monstrous anger of the guns.
Only the stuttering rifles' rapid rattle
Can patter out their hasty orisons.
No mockeries for them; no prayers nor bells,
   Nor any voice of mourning save the choirs,—
The shrill, demented choirs of wailing shells;
   And bugles calling for them from sad shires.

What candles may be held to speed them all?
   Not in the hands of boys, but in their eyes
Shall shine the holy glimmer of good-byes.
   The pallor of girls' brows shall be their pall;
Their flowers the tenderness of patient minds,
And each slow dusk a drawing-down of blinds.

WILFRED OWEN

▶ To His Love

Shall I compare thee to a summer's day?
Thou art more lovely and more temperate:
Rough winds do shake the darling buds of May,
And summer's lease hath all too short a date:
Sometime too hot the eye of heaven shines,
And often is his gold complexion dimm'd:
And every fair from fair sometime declines,
By chance, or nature's changing course, untrimm'd.
But thy eternal summer shall not fade
Nor lose possession of that fair thou owest;
Nor shall death brag thou wanderest in his shade,
When in eternal lines to time thou growest:
So long as men can breathe, or eyes can see,
So long lives this, and this gives life to thee.

WILLIAM SHAKESPEARE

INDEX OF FIRST LINES